Cadence

LUXE KNITS BY KNIT PICKS

Photography by John Cranford

Printed in the United States of America

First Printing, 2019

ISBN 978-1-62767-250-4

Versa Press, Inc.
800-447-7829

www.versapress.com

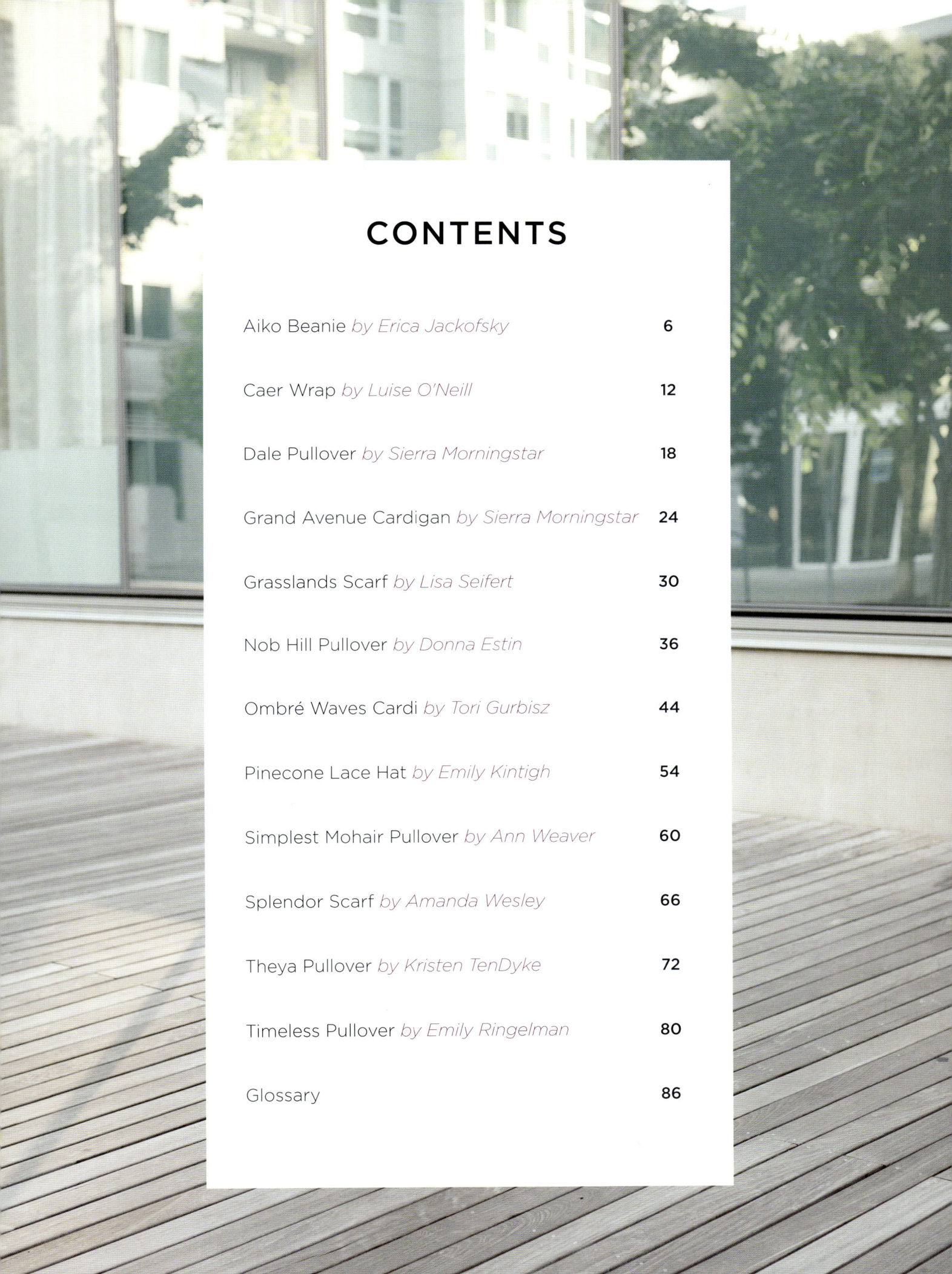

CONTENTS

AIKO BEANIE

by Erica Jackofsky

FINISHED MEASUREMENTS
16″ circumference, unstretched ×
9″ height

YARN
Knit Picks Capra™ (DK weight, 85%
Fine Merino Wool, 15% Cashmere; 123
yards/50g): Tansy Heather 27661, 2 balls

NEEDLES
US 4 (3.5mm) 16″ circular needles,
or size to obtain gauge
US 6 (4mm) 16″ circular needles,
plus DPNs or two 24″ circular needles
for two circulars technique, or size to
obtain gauge

NOTIONS
Yarn Needle
Stitch Marker

GAUGE
30 sts and 30 rnds = 4″ in 1x1 Rib in
the round on smaller needles, unblocked
and relaxed
24 sts and 24 rnds = approx 4″ in Aiko
Lace stitch in the round on larger
needles, blocked

Aiko Beanie

Notes:

This hat was inspired by the romantic texture and lace designs found in Japanese knitting. It seems fitting to give it the female Japanese name of Aiko.

The finished size given is measured with the ribbing relaxed. Hats should fit with negative ease, making the 16" relaxed rib circumference suitable for most adults.

The chart is worked in the round; read each row from right to left as a RS row.

DIRECTIONS

Ribbed Brim

With smaller needles, loosely CO 120 sts. PM and join for working in the rnd, being careful not to twist sts.
Work 1x1 Rib until piece measures 1.75" from CO edge.

Body

Change to larger needles. Begin Aiko Lace chart and rep chart six times per rnd, or work from written instructions as follows:

Rnd 1: *K1, (YO, K2tog) four times, YO, P1, (YO, SSK) four times, YO, K1, P1; rep from * five more times. 12 sts inc; 132 sts.

Rnd 2: (K10, P1) twelve times.

Rnd 3: *K1, (YO, K2tog) four times, YO, K1, P1, K1, (YO, SSK) four times, YO, K1, P1; rep from * five more times. 12 sts inc; 144 sts.

Rnd 4: (K11, P1) twelve times.

Rnd 5: *K1, (K2tog, YO) four times, K2, P1, K2, (YO, SSK) four times, K1, P1; rep from * five more times.

Rnd 6: Rep Rnd 4.

Rnd 7: *(K2tog, YO) four times, K3, P1, K3, (YO, SSK) four times, P1; rep from * five more times.

Rnd 8: Rep Rnd 4.

Rnd 9: *K1, (K2tog, YO) two times, K2tog, K4, YO, P1, YO, K4, (SSK, YO) two times, SSK, K1, P1; rep from * five more times.

Rnd 10: (K4, K2tog, K4, YO, K1, P1, K1, YO, K4, SSK, K4, P1) six times.

Rnd 11: (K3, K2tog, K4, YO, K2, P1, K2, YO, K4, SSK, K3, P1) six times.

Rnd 12: (K2, K2tog, K4, YO, K3, P1, K3, YO, K4, SSK, K2, P1) six times.

Rnd 13: (K1, K2tog, K4, YO, K4, P1, K4, YO, K4, SSK, K1, P1) six times.

Rnd 14: (K2tog, K4, YO, K5, P1, K5, YO, K4, SSK, P1) six times.

Rnd 15: (K5, K2tog, K4, YO, P1, YO, K4, SSK, K5, P1) six times.

Rnd 16: (K4, K2tog, K4, YO, K1, P1, K1, YO, K4, SSK, K4, P1) six times.

Rnd 17: (K3, K2tog, K4, YO, K2, P1, K2, YO, K4, SSK, K3, P1) six times.

Rnd 18: (K2, K2tog, K4, YO, K3, P1, K3, YO, K4, SSK, K2, P1) six times.

Rnd 19: (K1, K2tog, K4, YO, K4, P1, K4, YO, K4, SSK, K1, P1) six times.

Rnd 20: (K2tog, K4, YO, K5, P1, K5, YO, K4, SSK, P1) six times.

Rnd 21: Rep Rnd 4.

Rnd 22: *K1, (YO, SSK) three times, K4, P1, K4, (K2tog, YO) three times, K1, P1; rep from * five more times.

Rnd 23: Rep Rnd 4.

Rnd 24: *(YO, SSK) four times, K3, P1, K3, (K2tog, YO) four times, P1; rep from * five more times.

Rnd 25: Rep Rnd 4.

Rnd 26: *K1, (YO, SSK) four times, K2, P1, K2, (K2tog, YO) four times, K1, P1; rep from * five more times.

Rnd 27: Rep Rnd 4.

Crown

Begin Crown decreases. Change to DPNs when necessary.

Rnd 28: *(SSK, YO) four times, SSK, K1, P1, K1, (K2tog, YO) four times, K2tog, P1; rep from * five more times. 12 sts dec; 132 sts.

Rnd 29: (K10, P1) twelve times.

Rnd 30: *K2, (YO, SSK) four times, P1, (K2tog, YO) four times, K2, P1, M; rep from * five more times.

Rnd 31: Rep Rnd 29.

Rnd 32: *K1, (SSK, YO) three times, SSK, K1, P1, K1, (K2tog, YO) three times, K2tog, K1, P1; rep from * five more times. 12 sts dec; 120 sts.

Rnd 33: (K9, P1) twelve times.

Rnd 34: *K3, (YO, SSK) three times, P1, (K2tog, YO) three times, K3, P1; rep from * five more times.

Rnd 35: Rep Rnd 33.

Rnd 36: *K2, (SSK, YO) two times, SSK, K1, P1, K1, (K2tog, YO) two times, K2tog, K2, P1; rep from * five more times. 12 sts dec; 108 sts.

Rnd 37: (SSK, K6, P1, K6, K2tog, P1) six times. 12 sts dec; 96 sts.

Rnd 38: *SSK, K1, (YO, SSK) two times, P1, (K2tog, YO) two times, K1, K2tog, P1; rep from * five more times. 12 sts dec; 84 sts.

Rnd 39: (SSK, K4, P1, K4, K2tog, P1) six times. 12 sts dec; 72 sts.

Rnd 40: (SSK, YO, SSK, K1, P1, K1, K2tog, YO, K2tog, P1) six times. 12 sts dec; 60 sts.

Rnd 41: (SSK, K2, P1, K2, K2tog, P1) six times. 12 sts dec; 48 sts.

Rnd 42: (SSK, K1, P1, K1, K2tog, P1) six times. 12 sts dec; 36 sts.

Rnd 43: (SSK, P1, K2tog, P1) six times. 12 sts dec; 24 sts.

Rnd 44: (SK2P, P1) six times. 12 sts.

Break yarn and pull through remaining 12 sts on needles.

Finishing

Weave in ends and block upper lace portion as desired.

Aiko Lace

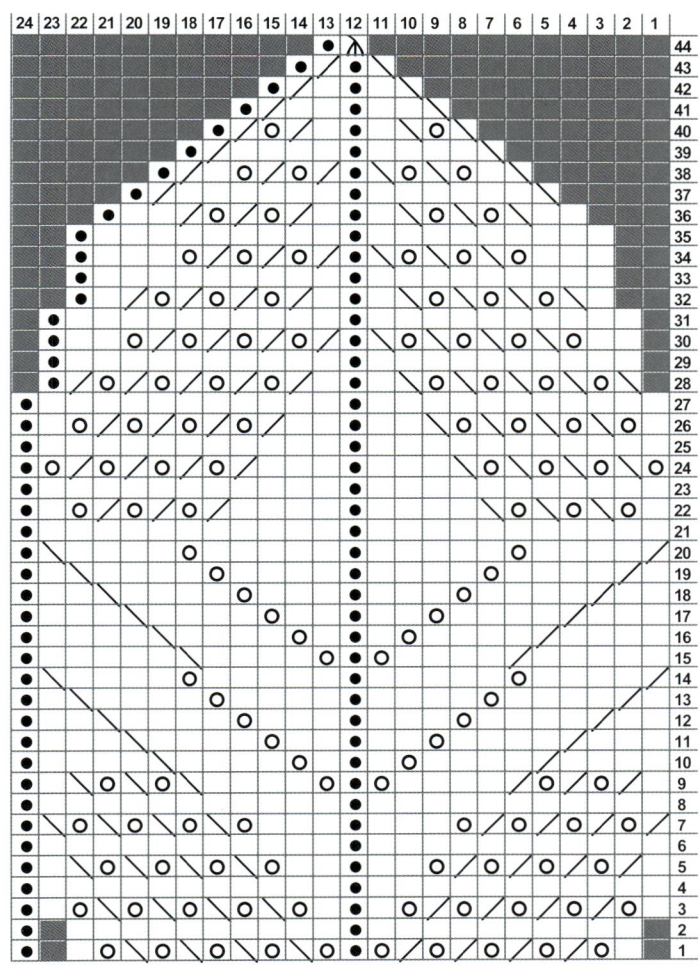

LEGEND

No Stitch
Placeholder—no stitch made

Knit Stitch

Purl Stitch

YO
Yarn over

K2tog
Knit 2 stitches together as one stitch

SSK
Slip, slip, knit slipped stitches together

SK2P
Slip 1 knit-wise, K2tog, pass slip stitch over K2tog

CAER WRAP

by Luise O'Neill

FINISHED MEASUREMENTS
26.5″ width × 84.5″ length

YARN
Knit Picks Andean Treasure™ (sport weight, 100% Baby Alpaca; 110 yards/50g): Embers Heather 23486, 10 balls

NEEDLES
US 10.5 (6.5mm) straight or circular needles, or size to obtain gauge

NOTIONS
Yarn Needle
Stitch Markers (optional)
Blocking Wires (optional)

GAUGE
12.75 sts and 17.75 rows = 4″ in Pattern Stitch, blocked

For pattern support, contact patternsupport@impeccableknits.ca

Caer Wrap

Notes:

Caer - The Dream Weaver is a gentle Celtic music piece by modern-day composer Peter Gundry. Like the music, gentle lines wander through the real and ethereal landscape creating a luxuriously dreamy wrap.

Caer is an extra-long, rectangular wrap that begins and ends with a narrow Garter Stitch border. The body of the wrap is worked in an eight-stitch pattern repeat that is bracketed by modified ribbed edges. Using larger needles than usually recommended for this yarn weight creates amazing drape in the fabric.

To adjust the width, note that each eight-stitch Caer Pattern repeat is 2.5" wide, blocked. To adjust to the length, each 16-row pattern stitch repeat is 3.5" long, blocked.

The chart is worked flat; read RS rows (odd numbers) from right to left, and WS rows (even numbers) from left to right.

Caer Pattern (worked flat over a multiple of 8 sts plus 9)
Row 1 (RS): Sl1 WYIF, K3, (P2, K2tog, YO, P1, YO, SSK, P1) to last 5 sts, P1, K4.
Row 2 (WS): Sl1 WYIB, (P1, K1) two times, *(K1, P2) two times, K2; rep from * to last 4 sts, P1, K1, P2.
Row 3: Sl1 WYIF, K3, (P1, K2tog, YO, K3, YO, SSK) to last 5 sts, P1, K4.
Row 4: Sl1 WYIB, (P1, K1) two times, (P7, K1) to last 4 sts, P1, K1, P2.
Row 5: Sl1 WYIF, K3, (P1, K7) to last 5 sts, P1, K4.
Row 6: Rep Row 4.
Row 7: Sl1 WYIF, K3, (P1, K1, K2tog, YO, P1, YO, SSK, K1) to last 5 sts, P1, K4.
Row 8: Sl1 WYIB, (P1, K1) two times, (P2, K3, P2, K1) to last 4 sts, P1, K1, P2.
Row 9: Sl1 WYIF, K3, (P1, YO, SSK, P3, K2tog, YO) to last 5 sts, P1, K4.
Row 10: Sl1 WYIB, P1, K1, P4, K3, (P5, K3) to last 7 sts, P4, K1, P2.
Row 11: Sl1 WYIF, K3, (K2, YO, SSK, P1, K2tog, YO, K1) to last 5 sts, K5.
Row 12: Sl1 WYIB, P1, K1, P5, K1, (P7, K1) to last 8 sts, P5, K1, P2.
Row 13: Sl1 WYIF, (K7, P1) to last 8 sts, K8.
Row 14: Rep Row 12.
Row 15: Sl1 WYIF, K3, (P1, YO, SSK, K1, P1, K1, K2tog, YO) to last 5 sts, P1, K4.
Row 16: Sl1 WYIB, (P1, K1) two times, *(K1, P2) two times, K2; rep from * to last 4 sts, P1, K1, P2.
Rep Rows 1-16 for pattern.

DIRECTIONS

Loosely CO 89 sts.
Row 1 (RS): K across.
Row 2 (WS): K across.

Work 16-row Caer Pattern from the chart or written directions a total of 24 times.
Next 2 Rows: K across.

BO loosely.
Break yarn leaving a 6" tail.

Finishing

Weave in ends, wash, and block to measurements.

LEGEND

☐	**K** RS: Knit stitch WS: Purl stitch
⊡	**P** RS: Purl stitch WS: Knit stitch
☑	**Sl WYIF** RS: Slip stitch purl-wise, with yarn in front WS: Slip stitch purl-wise, with yarn in back
⊙	**YO** Yarn over
◪	**K2tog** Knit 2 stitches together as one stitch
◩	**SSK** Slip, slip, knit slipped stitches together
☐	**Pattern Repeat**

Caer Pattern

DALE PULLOVER

by Sierra Morningstar

FINISHED MEASUREMENTS

33.5 (36.5, 39, 42, 45, 48, 52, 55.5)"
finished bust circumference; meant
to be worn with 2-4" positive ease

YARN

Knit Picks Andean Treasure™ (sport
weight, 100% Baby Alpaca; 110
yards/50g): Fog Heather 23490,
7 (8, 9, 10, 10, 12, 12, 13) balls

NEEDLES

US 6 (4mm) circular needles in length
to accommodate body stitches, plus
16" circular needles and DPNs, or size
to obtain gauge.

NOTIONS

Yarn Needle
10 Stitch Markers: 8 to mark Raglan
shaping & 2 to mark Lace
Scrap Yarn or Stitch Holder

GAUGE

21 sts and 30 rnds = 4" in Stockinette
Stitch in the round, blocked
19 sts and 30 rnds = 4" in Fountain Lace
pattern in the round, blocked

For pattern support, contact Morn5420@yahoo.com

Dale Pullover

Notes:

Like an English dale cutting through the landscape, a gentle lace panel travels down the front of this sweater. The fountain lace pattern evokes church steeples decorating the valley while the Andean Treasure is as soft as a gentle breeze from the hills.

Dale is knit in the round from the top down. The ribbing for the neck is worked first, and then the neckline is shaped with short rows worked across the back.

The chart is worked in the round; read each row from right to left as a RS row.

When working the ribbing, two markers are placed for each raglan seam and abbreviated as follows:

RB (right back raglan)
RF (right front raglan)
LB (left back raglan)
LF (left front raglan)

When working the raglan shaping, the first lace marker acts as the BOR marker. After separating the sleeves, a new marker is placed along the right-hand side to act as the BOR marker.

Knitted Cast On

A tutorial can be found at https://tutorials.knitpicks.com/knitted-cast-on.

Fountain Lace (in the round over a multiple of 4 sts plus 1)

Rnd 1: K1, (YO, K3, YO, K1) to end.
Rnd 2: K all.
Rnd 3: K2, SK2P, (K3, SK2P) to last 2 sts, K2.
Rnd 4: K all.
Rep Rnds 1-4 for pattern.

Allover Raglan Increase Pattern

Rnd 1: Work Fountain Lace to M, (K to M, M1R, SM, K1, SM, M1L) four times, K to end. 8 sts inc; 2 each for front, back, and shoulders.
Rnd 2: Work Fountain Lace as established to M, K to end.

Shoulder Raglan Increase Pattern

Rnd 1: Work Fountain Lace to M, (K to M, SM, K1, SM, M1L, K to M, M1R, SM, K1, SM) two times, K to end. 4 sts inc; 2 each for shoulders.
Rnd 2: Work Fountain Lace as established to M, K to end.

Body Raglan Increase Pattern

Rnd 1: Work Fountain Lace to M, (K to M, M1R, SM, K1, SM, K to M, SM, K1, SM, M1L) two times, K to end. 4 sts inc; 2 each for front and back.
Rnd 2: Work Fountain Lace as established to M, K to end.

DIRECTIONS

Neck

Using Long Tail Cast On or method of your choice and shorter circular needles, loosely CO 108 (116, 124, 124, 132, 132, 136, 144) sts. PM and join to work in the rnd, being careful not to twist sts. BOR will be back M of RB. Work 1x1 Rib for two rnds.

Next Rnd: Cont in 1x1 Rib; K1, PM (RB), work 11 (11, 11, 11, 11, 11, 11, 13) sts for right shoulder, PM, K1, PM, (RF), work 4 (4, 6, 6, 8, 8, 7, 8) sts, PM, work 33 (37, 37, 37, 37, 37, 37, 41) sts, PM, work 4 (4, 6, 6, 8, 8, 7, 8) sts, PM, K1, PM (LF), work 11 (11, 11, 11, 11, 11, 11, 13) sts for left shoulder, PM, K1, PM (LB), work to end.

Short Row Shaping

Change to St st, worked flat.
Setup Row (RS): Knit to 1 st after RF, W&T.

Short Row 1 (WS): P to 1 st after LF, W&T.
Short Row 2: (K to M, M1R, SM, K1, SM, M1L) four times, K to wrapped st from previous row, PU wrap and K tog with st, W&T. 8 sts inc.
Work Short Rows 1-2 1 (1, 1, 1, 1, 2, 2, 2) more times; on WS row reps, PU wrap and P tog with st then W&T next st. 124 (132, 140, 140, 148, 156, 160, 168) sts.
On last Short Row PU wrap from previous row and K to next M. This is new BOR.
Remainder of body is worked in the rnd.

Raglan Shaping

Setup Rnd: K all (PU remaining wrap from LF shoulder).
Raglan Inc Step 1: Work 2-row Allover Raglan Increase Pattern 19 (18, 20, 25, 25, 23, 23, 22) times.
Raglan Inc Step 2: Work 2-row Shoulder Raglan Increase Pattern 1 (1, 1, 0, 0, 0, 0, 0) times.
Raglan Inc Step 3: *Work 2-row Body Raglan Increase Pattern 0 (0, 0, 0, 1, 1, 1, 1) times, then work 2-row Allover Raglan Increase Pattern 0 (1, 1, 0, 0, 1, 1, 1) times; rep from * 0 (1, 1, 0, 0, 1, 3, 4) more times.

Size 36.5" Only

Work 2-row Allover Raglan Increase Pattern once more.

40 (46, 48, 50, 52, 54, 62, 64) rnds worked; 156 (176, 184, 200, 204, 208, 232, 236) sts inc; 280 (308, 324, 340, 352, 364, 392, 404) sts.

Divide for Body

Cont in Fountain Lace as established, work to LF, place next 57 (63, 65, 67, 67, 69, 73, 75) sts (raglan seam and sleeve sts) on st holder or scrap yarn; using Knitted Cast On, CO 3 (3, 3, 5, 7, 11, 11, 17) sts at left underarm, work across back to RB M, place next 57 (63, 65, 67, 67, 69, 73, 75) sts (raglan seam and sleeve stitches) on st holder or scrap yarn; CO 3 (3, 3, 5, 7, 11, 11, 17) sts at right underarm, placing a new M after the first 2 (2, 2, 3, 3, 5, 5, 7) CO sts. This is new BOR. 172 (188, 200, 216, 232, 248, 268, 288) sts for body.

Body

Next Rnd: Work in St st to M, work Fountain Lace pattern as established to next M, K to end.
Rep this rnd until piece measures 14.5" from underarm or desired length, ending on Fountain Lace Rnd 3 or 4.
Work 1x1 Rib for five rnds.
BO all sts.

Sleeves (make two the same)

Place held 57 (63, 65, 67, 67, 69, 73, 75) sleeve sts on shorter circular needles or DPNs.
From center st of underarm CO, PU and K 1 st, PM, PU and K 1 (1, 1, 2, 3, 5, 5, 8) from underarm, K across sleeve sts, PU and K 1 (1, 1, 2, 3, 5, 5, 8) from underarm, PM for BOR and join.
60 (66, 68, 72, 74, 80, 84, 92) sts.
Knit five rnds.

Dec Rnd: K1, SM, K2tog, K to last 2 sts, SSK. 2 sts dec.
Cont in St st, working Dec Rnd every 12 (11, 11, 9, 9, 8, 8, 7) rnds 8 (10, 10, 12, 12, 14, 14, 13) more times, then every 6 rnds 0 (0, 0, 0, 0, 0, 0, 4) times. 42 (44, 46, 46, 48, 50, 54, 56) sts.
Change to DPNs when necessary.

Work until sleeve measures 16.5 (17, 17, 17, 17, 17, 17.5, 17.5)".
Work 1x1 Rib for three rnds.
BO all sts.

Finishing

Weave in ends. Block to measurements.

Fountain Lace

7	6	5	4	3	2	1	
		■	⋏	■			4
		■	⋏	■			3
							2
	O				O		1

LEGEND

■ **No Stitch**
Placeholder—no stitch made

□ **Knit Stitch**

O **YO**
Yarn over

⋏ **SK2P**
Slip 1 knit-wise, K2tog, pass slip stitch over K2tog

□ **Pattern Repeat**

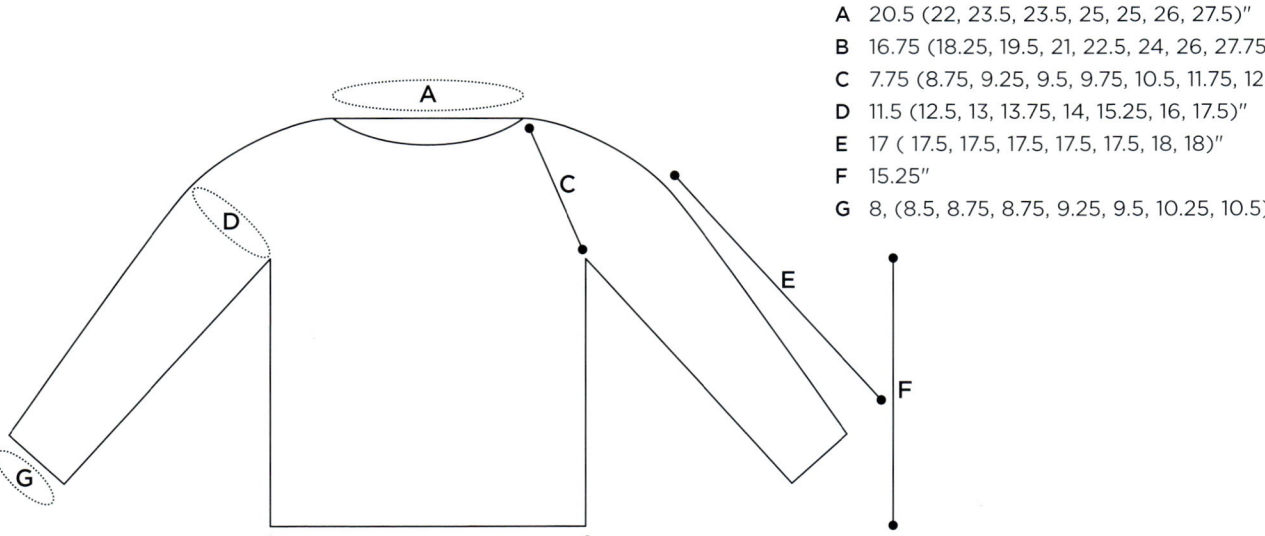

A   20.5 (22, 23.5, 23.5, 25, 25, 26, 27.5)"
B   16.75 (18.25, 19.5, 21, 22.5, 24, 26, 27.75)"
C   7.75 (8.75, 9.25, 9.5, 9.75, 10.5, 11.75, 12.75)"
D   11.5 (12.5, 13, 13.75, 14, 15.25, 16, 17.5)"
E   17 (17.5, 17.5, 17.5, 17.5, 17.5, 18, 18)"
F   15.25"
G   8, (8.5, 8.75, 8.75, 9.25, 9.5, 10.25, 10.5)"

GRAND AVENUE CARDIGAN

by Sierra Morningstar

FINISHED MEASUREMENTS

33 (36.25, 39.5, 42.5, 45, 49, 52.25, 55.5)″ finished bust circumference; meant to be worn open with 2-4″ positive ease

YARN

Knit Picks Paragon™ (sport weight, 50% Fine Merino Wool, 25% Baby Alpaca, 25% Mulberry Silk; 123 yards/50g): Kenai 26966, 9 (10, 11, 12, 13, 13, 14, 15) balls

NEEDLES

US 6 (4mm) circular needles long enough to accommodate bottom circumference, plus 16″ circular needles and DPNs, or size to obtain gauge

NOTIONS

Yarn Needle
Stitch Markers
Scrap Yarn or Stitch Holders

GAUGE

20 sts and 32 rows = 4″ in Stockinette Stitch worked flat, blocked
22 sts and 32 rows = 4″ in 2x2 Rib worked flat, blocked
28 sts and 32 rows = 4″ in Wrapped Rib Pattern, blocked

For pattern support, contact Morn5420@yahoo.com

Grand Avenue Cardigan

Notes:

Inspired by the striped awnings of Grand Hotel on Mackinac Island, a wrapped rib band decorates the edges of this cardigan, while the A-line shape hangs gracefully around the body.

This open-front cardigan is knit from the bottom up then divided at the underarm and worked separately to the shoulders. The front band is knit at the same time as the body, then continued past the shoulders to meet at the back neck. Set-in sleeves are worked in the round from the top down and shaped with short rows.

The front edge stitch is worked in Stockinette Stitch, and slipped at the beginning of every row.

The chart is worked flat; read RS rows (odd numbers) from right to left, and WS rows (even numbers) from left to right.

Wrap 4
WYIB, insert RH needle from front to back in between the fourth and fifth sts on LH needle, wrap working yarn around needle, and pull through to front; place loop on LH needle and P tog with next st.

Wrapped Rib (worked flat over a multiple of 4 sts plus 2)
Row 1 (RS): P1, (Wrap 4, K2, P1) to last st, P1.
Row 2 (WS): (K2, P2) to last 2 sts, K2.
Row 3: P2, (K2, P2) to end.
Row 4: Rep Row 2.
Rep Rows 1-4 for pattern.

DIRECTIONS

Hem
Using Long Tail Cast On or method of your choice, CO 216 (232, 248, 264, 280, 304, 320, 336) sts.
Setup Row (RS): Sl1 WYIB, P2, (K2, P2) six times, PM, work 2x2 Rib and PM after 30 (34, 38, 42, 46, 52, 56, 60) sts, cont 2x2 Rib for 102 (110, 118, 126, 134, 146, 154, 162) sts, PM, cont for 30 (34, 38, 42, 46, 52, 56, 60) sts, PM, P2, (K2, P2) six times, K1.

LEGEND

	K RS: Knit stitch WS: Purl stitch		P RS: Purl stitch WS: Knit stitch

Wrap 4
WYIB, insert RH needle from front to back, in between the 4th and 5th st on LH needle, wrap working yarn around needle and pull through to front, place loop on LH needle and P tog with next st

Pattern Repeat

Wrapped Rib

Bottom Rib
Next Row (WS): Sl1 WYIF, starting with Row 2, work Wrapped Rib to M, SM, work 2x2 Rib to last M, SM, work Wrapped Rib to last st, P1.

Continuing to keep both edge sts in St st, and slipping first st of every row, WE as established until piece measures 2" from CO edge, ending on a WS row.

Body
Setup Dec Row (RS): Sl1 WYIB, work Wrapped Rib to M, SM, change to St st and dec 2 (2, 2, 2, 3, 4, 4, 4) sts evenly spaced to 2 sts before M, SSK, SM, K2tog, dec 8 (8, 8, 8, 10, 12, 12, 12) sts evenly spaced to 2 sts before next M, SSK, SM, K2tog, dec 2 (2, 2, 2, 3, 4, 4, 4) sts evenly spaced to next M, work Wrapped Rib to M, K1. 16 (16, 16, 16, 20, 24, 24, 24) sts dec; 200 (216, 232, 248, 260, 280, 296, 312) sts divided as follows for the Right Front / Back / Left Front: 54/92/54 (58/100/58, 62/108/62, 66/116/66, 69/122/69, 74/132/74, 78/140/78, 82/148/82).
WE as established until piece measures 3" from CO edge, ending with a WS row.
Dec Row (RS): WE to 2 sts before first side M, SSK, SM, K2tog, K to next M, SSK, SM, K2tog, work as established to end. 4 sts dec.
Cont in pattern as established, working Dec Row every 3", four more times. 180 (196, 212, 228, 240, 260, 276, 292) sts.
WE as established until piece measures 16" from CO edge, ending with a WS row.

Divide for Front & Back
Removing side Ms when reached, work 46 (49, 52, 55, 56, 60, 63, 66) sts, place sts just worked on st holder or scrap yarn for Right Front, BO 6 (8, 10, 12, 16, 18, 20, 22) sts, K76 (82, 88, 94, 96, 104, 110, 116) and place sts just worked on holder for Back, BO 6 (8, 10, 12, 16, 18, 20, 22) sts, work as established to end of row. 168 (180, 192, 204, 208, 224, 236, 248) sts total; 46 (49, 52, 55, 56, 60, 63, 66) sts on needle.

Left Front
Next Row (WS): WE as established.
Dec Row (RS): K1, K2tog, work to end. 1 st dec.
Rep Dec Row every RS row 1 (2, 3, 5, 4, 7, 9, 11) more times. 44 (46, 48, 49, 51, 52, 53, 54) sts.
WE until armhole measures 6.5 (7, 7.5, 8, 8.5, 9.5, 10, 11.5)", ending on a WS row.

Shape Shoulder
At beginning of next RS row BO 8 (8, 10, 10, 12, 12, 12, 12) sts; at beginning of next RS row BO 4 (6, 6, 6, 6, 7, 7, 8) sts; at beginning of next RS row BO 5 (5, 5, 6, 6, 6, 7, 7) sts, removing M on final row. 27 sts.

Cont to work Wrapped Rib band until piece measures 3.75"
past shoulder BO.
BO all sts.

Back
Return 76 (82, 88, 94, 96, 104, 110, 116) held Back sts to
needles and join yarn with WS facing.
Next Row (WS): P across.
Dec Row (RS): K1, K2tog, K to last 3 sts, SSK, K1. 2 sts dec.
Rep Dec Row every RS row 1 (2, 3, 5, 4, 7, 9, 11) more times.
72 (76, 80, 82, 86, 88, 90, 92) sts.
WE in St st until armhole measures 6.5 (7, 7.5, 8, 8.5, 9.5, 10,
11.5)", ending with a WS row.

Shape Shoulder
Next Row: At beginning of next two rows BO 8 (8, 10, 10, 12,
12, 12, 12) sts; then at beginning of next two rows BO 4 (6, 6,
6, 6, 7, 7, 8) sts; then at beginning of next two rows BO 5 (5,
5, 6, 6, 6, 7, 7) sts.
BO remaining 38 sts.

Right Front
Return 46 (49, 52, 55, 56, 60, 63, 66) held Right Front sts
to needles and join yarn with WS facing.
Next Row (WS): WE as established.
Dec Row (RS): Work to last 3 sts, SSK, K1. 1 st dec.
Rep Dec Row every RS row 1 (2, 3, 5, 4, 7, 9, 11) more times.
44 (46, 48, 49, 51, 52, 53, 54) sts.
WE until armhole measures 6.5 (7, 7.5, 8, 8.5, 9.5, 10, 11.5)",
ending on a RS row.

Shape Shoulder
At beginning of next WS row BO 8 (8, 10, 10, 12, 12, 12, 12) sts;
at beginning of next WS row BO 4 (6, 6, 6, 6, 7, 7, 8) sts; at
beginning of next WS row BO 5 (5, 5, 6, 6, 6, 7, 7) sts. 27 sts.
Cont to work Wrapped Rib band until piece measures 3.75"
past shoulder BO.
BO all sts.

Sleeves (make two the same)
Sew shoulder seams.
With 16" circular needles and starting at center underarm,
PU and K 3 (4, 5, 6, 8, 9, 10, 11) sts (one from each underarm
BO st), PU and K 29 (30, 31, 32, 33, 37, 38, 39) sts from side
of armhole, PM for center, PU and K 29 (30, 31, 32, 33, 37, 38,
39) sts from other side, then PU and K 3 (4, 5, 6, 8, 9, 10, 11)
sts (one from each underarm BO st). 64 (68, 72, 76, 82, 92,
96, 100) sts.

Short Rows
Short Row 1 (RS): K43 (45, 48, 50, 52, 61, 64, 66), W&T.
Short Row 2 (WS): P to 10 (11, 12, 12, 13, 15, 16, 16) sts past
center shoulder M, W&T.
Short Row 3: K to 1 st past wrapped st from previous row,
PU wrap and K tog with st, W&T.
Short Row 4: P to 1 st past wrapped st from previous row,
PU wrap and P tog with st, W&T.
Rep Short Rows 3-4 until 3 (4, 5, 6, 8, 9, 10, 11) sts remain
to center M. On final RS row, PU wrap from previous row
and K tog with st then work to end of row, PM for BOR.
Begin working in the rnd. Knit two rnds (PU final wrap
and K tog with st on the first rnd).

Sleeve Shaping
Dec Rnd: K2tog, K to last 2 sts, SSK. 2 sts dec.
Cont in St st, work Dec Row every 9 (9, 9, 8, 8, 6, 6, 6) rnds a
total of 12 (12, 12, 14, 15, 20, 20, 20) times. 40 (44, 48, 48, 52,
52, 56, 60) sts.
WE until sleeve measures 14.75 (15, 15, 15, 15.5, 15.5, 15.5,
15.5)" from underarm, changing to DPNs when necessary.
Work 2x2 Rib for 2".
BO all sts.

Finishing
Weave in ends, wash, and block to diagram.
Sew neck extensions together at back of neck. Sew edge
of neck band to the top of back of neck.

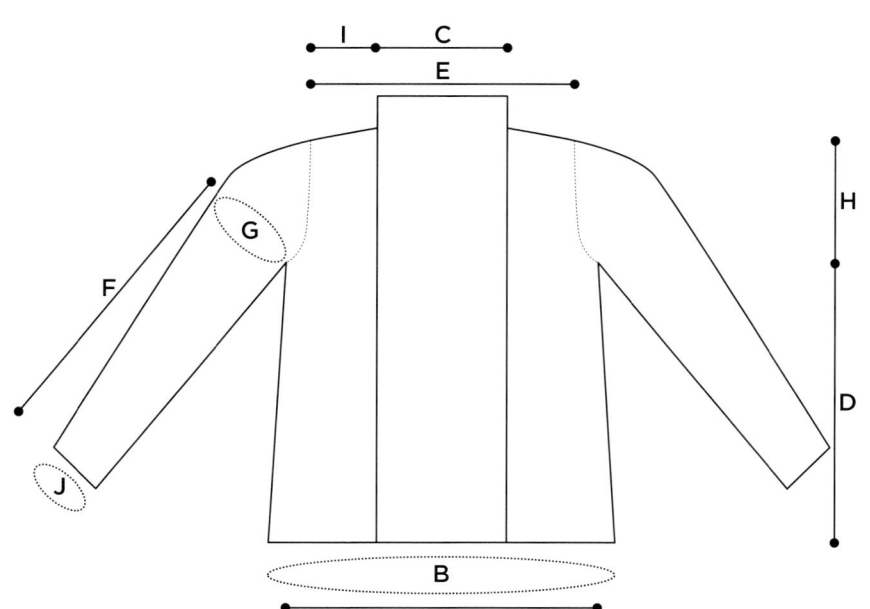

A 16.5 (18, 19.5, 21, 22.5, 24.5, 26, 27.5)"
B 37.25 (40, 43, 46, 48.75, 53.25, 56, 59)"
C 7.5"
D 16"
E 14.5 (15.25, 16, 16.5, 17.25, 17.5, 18, 18.5)"
F 16.75 (17, 17, 17, 17.5, 17.5, 17.5, 17.5)"
G 12.75, (13.5, 14.5, 15.25, 16.5, 18.5, 19.25, 20)"
H 6.5 (7, 7.5, 8, 8.5, 9.5, 10, 11.5)"
I 3.5 (3.75, 4.25, 4.5, 4.75, 5, 5.25, 5.5)"
J 7.25 (8, 8.75, 8.75, 9.5, 9.5, 10.25, 11)"

GRASSLANDS SCARF

by Lisa Seifert

FINISHED MEASUREMENTS
14.5″ width × 70″ length, excluding fringe

YARN
Knit Picks Andean Treasure™ (sport weight, 100% Baby Alpaca; 110 yards/50g): Sapphire Heather 24624, 7 balls

NEEDLES
US 5 (3.75mm) straight or circular needles, or size to obtain gauge

NOTIONS
Yarn Needle
Stitch Markers
Crochet Hook (for fringe)

GAUGE
21 sts and 28 rows = 4″ in Grasslands Stitch Pattern, blocked

For pattern support, contact happyindolevalley@gmail.com

Grasslands Scarf

Notes:

Reflecting the chill of a breeze through autumn grasses, Grasslands is a luxurious accessory with an unassuming, subtle texture that lets the oh-so-soft baby alpaca do the talking.

The Grasslands Scarf is generously sized and doubles as a wrap. Worked flat from the short end with an easily memorized stitch pattern, a garter stitch border, and finished with a flirty fringe, Grasslands is engaging for knitters of all skill levels.

When joining new yarn, work two knit or purl stitches holding both old and new yarn strands together; avoid working joins over Grass-Stitches.

GS (Grass-Stitch)
Sl1 P-wise, K1, YO, PSSO.

Grasslands Stitch Pattern (worked flat)
Row 1 (WS): K3, SM, P to last 3 sts, SM, K3.
Row 2 (RS): K3, SM, (K2, GS) to 2 sts before M, K2, SM, K3.
Rep Rows 1-2 for pattern.

DIRECTIONS
Loosely CO 76 sts.
Setup Row (RS): K3, PM, K to last 3 sts, PM, K3.
Rows 1-4: Work Garter st for four rows.
Row 5 (WS): Work Grasslands Stitch Pattern Row 1.
Row 6 (RS): Work Grasslands Stitch Pattern Row 2.
Rows 7-460: Rep Rows 5-6 227 times.
Rows 461-464: Work Garter st for four rows.
BO loosely on WS, break yarn.

Finishing
Weave in ends, wash, and block to finished measurements.

Fringe
Cut 76 fringe pieces to lengths of 10.5". Fold single strands in half and using crochet hook attach 38 strands evenly across each end of scarf.

NOB HILL PULLOVER

by Donna Estin

FINISHED MEASUREMENTS

30 (34, 38, 42, 46, 50)″ finished bust circumference; meant to be worn with 1-2″ positive ease

YARN

Knit Picks Alpaca Cloud™ (fingering weight, 100% Superfine Alpaca; 200 yards/50g): Elizabeth 26874 6 (6, 7, 8, 9, 10) hanks

NEEDLES

US 2 (2.75mm) DPNs and 24″ circular needles, or size to obtain gauge

US 1 (2.25mm) 24″ circular needles, or one size smaller than size used to obtain gauge

NOTIONS

Yarn Needle
Stitch Markers

GAUGE

26 sts and 44 rnds = 4″ in Madeira Lace Pattern in the round on larger needles, blocked
29 sts and 44 rnds = 4″ in Stockinette Stitch in the round, blocked

For pattern support, contact donnaestindesigns@gmail.com

Nob Hill Pullover

Notes:

The Nob Hill Pullover combines luxurious Alpaca Cloud yarn with an edgy design, proving that luxury is always redefining itself. A continuous lace panel encircles the body then changes direction and provides more coverage where you need it. Asymmetrical bands of Garter Stitch and eyelets wrap around the sleeves and neckline for fun accents.

This standard fitting pullover is worked in the round from the bottom up to the armholes, then divided and worked flat. Set in sleeves are worked in the round to the armholes then worked flat through the sleeve cap. The neckline is finished with a delicate I-Cord Bind Off.

Madeira Lace (in the round over a multiple of 8 sts plus 9)
Rnd 1: (YO, SSK, K6) to last st, K1.
Rnd 2: (K1, YO, SSK, K3, K2tog, YO) to last st, K1.
Rnd 3: (K2, YO, SSK, K1, K2tog, YO, K1) to last st, K1.
Rnd 4: (K3, YO, SK2P, YO, K2) to last st, K1.
Rnd 5: (K4, YO, SSK, K2) to last st, K1.
Rnd 6: (K2, K2tog, YO, K1, YO, SSK, K1) to last st, K1.
Rnd 7: (K1, K2tog, YO, K3, YO, SSK) to last st, K1.
Rnd 8: K2tog, YO, K5, YO, (SK2P, YO, K5, YO) to last 2 sts, SSK.
Rep Rnds 1-8 for pattern.

Diagonal Stitch (in the round over a multiple of 6 sts)
Rnd 1: (K4, P2) to end.
Rnd 2: (K3, P2, K1) to end.
Rnd 3: (K2, P2, K2) to end.
Rnd 4: (K1, P2, K3) to end.
Rnd 5: (P2, K4) to end.
Rnd 6: (P1, K4, P1) to end.
Rep Rnds 1-6 for pattern.

Diagonal Stitch (worked flat over a multiple of 6 sts)
Row 1 (RS): (K4, P2) to end.
Row 2 (WS): (P1, K2, P3) to end.
Row 3: (K2, P2, K2) to end.
Row 4: (P3, K2, P1) to end.
Row 5: (P2, K4) to end.
Row 6: (K1, P4, K1) to end.
Rep Rows 1-6 for pattern.

Eyelet Band (in the round over an even number of sts)
Rnd 1: P all.
Rnd 2: K all.
Rnds 3-4: Rep Rnds 1-2.
Rnd 5: (YO, K2tog) to end.
Rnds 6-8: Rep Rnds 2-4.
Rnd 9: P all.

I-Cord Bind Off
Setup Step: With RS facing, K first st but don't remove LH needle; turn RH needle clockwise and insert LH needle from left to right into st on RH needle; remove RH needle. 1 st CO. Rep Setup Step two more times. 3 sts CO.

I-Cord BO Step: K2, K2tog TBL, transfer 3 sts from RH to LH needle by slipping LH needle tip into all three sts from left to right; pull yarn snug.
Rep I-Cord BO Step until 3 sts remain.
Finishing Step: K2, *lift right st on RH needle over left st and off needle*, K1; rep between * and *.

DIRECTIONS

Body

Lower Lace Section
With larger circular needles, CO 218 (247, 276, 305, 334, 363) sts, PM, join in the rnd, being careful not to twist sts. Work Garter st for 1".
Dec Rnd: K2tog 1 (0, 0, 0, 0, 0) times, K1 (3, 0, 3, 0, 3), K2tog 1 (1, 0, 0, 0, 0) times, *K7 (6, 6, 5, 7, 6), K2tog, K8 (7, 0, 6, 0, 7), K2tog 1 (1, 0, 1, 0, 1) times; rep from * 10 (13, 33, 19, 36, 20) more times, K1 (1, 2, 2, 1, 3), K2tog 1 (1, 1, 0, 0, 0) times, K1 (1, 0, 0, 0, 0). 25 (30, 35, 40, 37, 42) sts dec; 193 (217, 241, 265, 297, 321) sts.
Work Madeira Lace until piece measures 10 (10, 10, 10.5, 11, 11)", when stretched lengthwise.

Upper Diagonal Section
Inc Rnd: K3 (3, 2, 2, 2, 3), M1 1 (1, 1, 1, 1, 0) times, *K8 (7, 7, 6, 8, 7), M1, K9 (8, 7, 7, 7, 0), M1 1 (1, 1, 1, 1, 0) times; rep from * 10 (13, 16, 19, 18, 44) more times, K3 (4, 1, 3, 10, 3). 23 (29, 35, 41, 39, 45) sts inc; 216 (246, 276, 306, 336, 366) sts.
Next Rnd: K108 (123, 138, 153, 168, 183), PM, K108 (123, 138, 153, 168, 183).
Next Rnd: *K42 (39, 42, 39, 42, 39), PM, work in Diagonal Stitch to M; rep from * to BOR.
Cont as established through Rnd 5 of Diagonal Stitch.
Rnd 6: *K to 1 st before M, P1, remove M, work in pattern to next M; rep from * to BOR.
Work in St st until 1 st remains before P st, P2, K4, cont in Diagonal Stitch as established to end.
Work like this, allowing Diagonal Stitch pattern to move 1 st to the right on every rnd until Diagonal Stitch fills body. Work all sts in Diagonal Stitch until section measures 5" from Inc Rnd; work a final partial rnd, stopping 2 (6, 8, 10, 10, 10) sts before first M.

Divide for Armholes
BO 4 (12, 16, 20, 20, 20) sts, cont in pattern to 2 (6, 8, 10, 10, 10) sts before BOR, BO 4 (12, 16, 20, 20, 20) sts. 104 (111, 122, 133, 148, 163) sts remain for each Back and Front. Leave Front sts on needles. Work flat, back and forth, for Back and Front sections.

Back
Row 1 (RS): Cont to work in Diagonal Stitch, maintaining pattern as established.
Row 2 (WS): WE in Diagonal Stitch across row.
Dec Row (RS): K1, SSK, work as established to last 3 sts, K2tog, K1. 2 sts dec; 102 (109, 120, 131, 146, 161) sts.

Next Row (WS): WE in Diagonal Stitch.

Rep Dec Row every RS row 0 (1, 3, 6, 10, 14) more times. 102 (107, 114, 119, 126, 133) sts.

Cont to WE as established until armhole measures 3.5 (4, 4, 4.5, 4.5, 5)", ending with a WS row.

Transition to St st

Transition Row 1 (RS): Work in pattern until you've worked the last purl st of this row, PM, K to end.

Transition Row 2 (WS): P to M, remove M, P1, K2, P4, cont in pattern to end.

Rep Transition Rows 1-2, allowing Diagonal Stitch to cont its course toward RH side of piece without introducing any new purl sts on LH side. When armhole measures 6.25 (6.75, 7.25, 7.75, 8.25, 8.75)", end with a WS row.

Shape Neck

Setup Row (RS): Work as established across 21 (23, 26, 28, 30, 32) sts, join second ball of yarn and BO center 60 (61, 62, 63, 66, 69) sts, work as established to end.

Next Row (WS): WE as established across both shoulders.

Dec Row (RS): Work as established to 3 sts before neck opening, K2tog, K1; with second ball, K1, SSK, work as established to end. 1 st dec on each side; 20 (22, 25, 27, 29, 31) sts per shoulder.

Next Row (WS): WE across both shoulders.

Rep Dec Row once. 19 (21, 24, 26, 28, 30) sts per shoulder.

Cont to WE until armhole measures 7.25 (7.75, 8.25, 8.75, 9.25, 9.75)", ending with a WS row.

Shape Shoulders

BO 10 (11, 12, 13, 14, 15) sts at beginning of next two rows (outer sides of each shoulder).

BO remaining 9 (10, 12, 13, 14, 15) sts per shoulder at beginning of next two rows.

Front

Rejoin yarn to begin a RS row. Work same as Back until armhole measures 5.25 (5.75, 6.25, 6.75, 7.25, 7.75)", ending with a WS row. 102 (107, 114, 119, 126, 133) sts.

Shape Neck

Setup Row (RS): Work as established across 35 (37, 40, 42, 45, 48) sts, join second ball of yarn and BO center 32 (33, 34, 35, 36, 37) sts, work as established to end.

Next Row (WS): WE as established across both shoulders.

Next 2 Rows: WE across first shoulder; BO 4 (4, 4, 4, 5, 6) sts at beginning of neck edge, then work to end.

Next 4 Rows: WE across first shoulder; BO 4 sts at beginning of neck edge, then work to end. (8 sts BO each shoulder.)

Next 4 Rows: WE across first shoulder; BO 2 sts at beginning of neck edge, then work to end. (4 sts BO each shoulder.) 19 (21, 24, 26, 28, 30) sts remain per shoulder.

Cont to WE across both shoulders until armhole measures 7.25 (7.75, 8.25, 8.75, 9.25, 9.75)", ending with a WS row.

Shape Shoulders

BO 10 (11, 12, 13, 14, 15) sts at beginning of next two rows (outer sides of each shoulder). BO remaining 9 (10, 12, 13, 14, 15) sts per shoulder at beginning of next two rows.

Left Sleeve

With DPNs, CO 66 (66, 66, 72, 72, 72) sts onto larger needles, distribute evenly and join in the rnd, being careful not to twist sts; PM for BOR.

Work Garter st for 1".

Work St st until sleeve measures 3".

Eyelet Band and incs are worked at the same time—read through section before beginning.

Inc Rnd: To keep incs aligned, work them at end of one rnd/beginning of next rnd as follows: K until 1 st before M, M1L, K1, SM, K1, M1R. 2 sts inc; 68 (68, 68, 74, 74, 74) sts.

Rep Inc Rnd every 20 (14, 12, 12, 8, 6) rnds 7 (10, 12, 3, 11, 19) more times, and every following 0 (0, 0, 14, 10, 8) rnds 0 (0, 0, 8, 6, 5) times. 82 (88, 92, 96, 108, 122) sts.

AT THE SAME TIME, when sleeve measures 11" work Eyelet Band over 9 rnds.

Cont inc as established and work in St st until sleeve measures 18 (18, 18, 18.5, 18.5, 19)", stopping last rnd 2 (6, 8, 10, 10, 10) sts before M.

Work remainder of sleeve flat, back and forth.

Shape Sleeve Cap

BO 4 (12, 16, 20, 20, 20) sts. 78 (76, 76, 76, 88, 102) sts.

Row 1 (RS): K across.

Row 2 (WS): P across.

BO 1 st at beginning of next 42 (32, 26, 20, 36, 54) rows. 36 (44, 50, 56, 52, 48) sts.

WE for two rows.

Dec Row (RS): K1, SSK, K to last 3 sts, K2tog, K1. 2 sts dec. 34 (42, 48, 54, 50, 46) sts.

Rep Dec Row every four rows 1 (4, 7, 9, 6, 2) more times. 32 (34, 34, 36, 38, 42) sts.

BO 3 sts at beginning of next two rows.

BO 2 sts at beginning of next four rows.

BO remaining 18 (20, 20, 22, 24, 28) sts.

Right Sleeve

Work same as Left Sleeve, with the exception of working two eyelet bands.

While working incs, AT THE SAME TIME, when sleeve measures 6" work Eyelet Band over 9 rnds.

Cont inc as established and work in St st until sleeve measures 15", work Eyelet Band over 9 rnds.

Cont inc as established and work in St st until sleeve measures 18 (18, 18, 18.5, 18.5, 19)", stopping last rnd 2 (6, 8, 10, 10, 10) sts before M.

Work remainder of sleeve flat, back and forth. Shape Right Sleeve cap as for Left Sleeve.

Finishing

Weave in ends. Wash and block to diagram. For blocking, lay body flat and pin everything in place except Madeira Lace. Place pins carefully along bottom of the diagonal pattern, stretch lace out to schematic measurements and pin in place. This keeps the lace opened up without interfering with the rest of the garment.

Sew shoulder seams. Set in sleeves.

Eyelet Neckband

With smaller needles and RS facing, begin at left shoulder seam and PU and K 146 (150, 142, 142, 160, 162) sts evenly around neck, PM, join in the rnd. Work Eyelet Band pattern for 9 rnds.

Knit one rnd.

BO all sts using I-Cord Bind Off.

Weave in remaining ends.

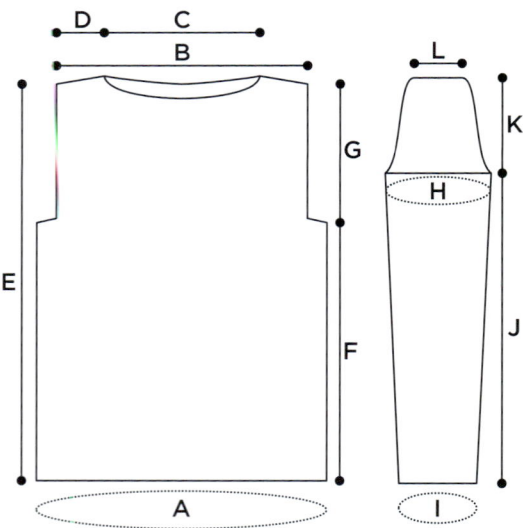

A   30 (34, 38, 42, 46, 50)"
B   12 (14.75, 15.75, 16.5, 17.5, 18.25)"
C   8.75 (9, 9.25, 9.25, 9.75, 10)"
D   2.5 (3, 3.25, 3.5, 3.75, 4.25)"
E   22.5 (23, 23.5, 24.5, 25.5, 26)"
F   15 (15, 15, 15.5, 16, 16)"
G   7.25 (7.75, 8.25, 8.75, 9.25, 9.75)"
H   11.25 (12.25, 12.75, 13.25, 15, 16.75)"
I   9 (9, 9, 10, 10, 10)"
J   18 (18, 18, 18.5, 18.5, 19)"
K   5.25 (5.5, 6, 6.25, 6.5, 6.75)"
L   2.5 (2.75, 2.75, 3, 3.25, 3.75)"

OMBRÉ WAVES CARDI

by Tori Gurbisz

FINISHED MEASUREMENTS

33.5 (38, 42.5, 45.75, 49.5, 54, 58.25)" finished bust circumference, buttoned; meant to be worn with 2-4" positive ease

YARN

Knit Picks Gloss™ (lace weight, 70% Merino Wool, 30% Silk; 440 yards/50g): MC Blackberry 27706, 5 (5, 6, 6, 7, 7, 8) hanks; C1 Sterling 24182, C2 Velveteen 27709, 1 (1, 1, 1, 1, 2, 2) hanks each

NEEDLES

US 7 (4.5mm) 24" or longer circular needles, plus DPNs or two 24" circular needles for two circulars technique or 32" or longer circular needles for Magic Loop technique, or size to obtain gauge

US 6 (4mm) 24" or longer circular needles, plus DPNs or two 24" circular needles for two circulars technique or 32" or longer circular needles for Magic Loop technique, or one size smaller than size used to obtain gauge

NOTIONS

Yarn Needle
Stitch Markers
Scrap Yarn or Stitch Holder
Eight Buttons, 0.75" in diameter

GAUGE

22 sts and 30 rows = 4" in Stockinette Stitch on larger needles with yarn held double, blocked

For pattern support, contact lachesisandco@gmail.com

Ombré Waves Cardi

Notes:

This design is inspired by colorful yokes and gradient knits. Both are easily and beautifully combined in this cardigan that you will love to knit and wear.

The Ombré Waves Cardi is worked flat from the top down with lace weight yarn held double. Alternating the colors held together creates the gradient yoke.

The chart is worked flat; read RS rows (odd numbers) from right to left, and WS rows (even numbers) from left to right.

M1L-P (make 1 left-leaning stitch purl-wise)
PU bar between st just worked and next st, and place on LH needle mounted as a regular knit st; purl through back loop.

M1R-P (make 1 right-leaning stitch purl-wise)
PU bar between st just worked and next st, and place on LH needle backwards (twisted st mount); purl through front.

Wave Pattern (worked flat over a multiple of 17 sts)
Row 1 (RS): *(K2tog) three times, (YO, K1) five times, YO, (SSK) three times; rep from * to end.
Rows 2-3: P across.

DIRECTIONS

Back
With larger circular needles and C1 held double, using Long Tail Cast On, CO 93 (106, 121, 127, 140, 150, 161) sts.

Wave One
Rows 1-9: Work St st.

Sizes 33.5 (38, 42.5, 45.75, 49.5, -, 58.25)" Only
Row 10, Wave Row (RS): K4 (2, 1, 4, 2, -, 4), work Wave Pattern Row 1 to last 4 (2, 1, 4, 2, -, 4) sts, K4 (2, 1, 4, 2, -, 4).

Size 54" Only
Row 10, Wave Row (RS): K3, YO, K2, SSK, work Wave Pattern Row 1 to last 7 sts, K2tog, K2, YO, K3.

Resume All Sizes
Rows 11-12: Work Wave Pattern Rows 2-3. Break one strand C1.

Wave Two
With one strand C1 and one strand C2 held tog, work twelve rows as for Wave One. Break C1.

Wave Three
With C2 held double, work twelve rows as for Wave One. Break one strand C2.

Wave Four
With one strand C2 and one strand MC held tog, work twelve rows as for Wave One. Break C2.

With MC held double, WE in St st until piece measures 7.5 (8, 8.5, 9, 9.25, 9.75, 9.75)", ending with a WS row.
Place sts on st holder or scrap yarn. Break yarn.

Wave Pattern

	17	16	15	14	13	12	11	10	9	8	7	6	5	4	3	2	1	
	●	●	●	●	●	●	●	●	●	●	●	●	●	●	●	●	●	3
2																		
	\	\	\	O		O		O		O		O		O	/	/	/	1

LEGEND

	K		P
☐	RS: Knit stitch WS: Purl stitch	●	RS: Purl stitch WS: Knit stitch

O — YO
Yarn over

⟋ — K2tog
Knit 2 stitches together as one stitch

⟍ — SSK
Slip, slip, knit slipped stitches together

Right Front
With RS facing, larger circular needles, and C1 held double, PU and K 25 (31, 36, 39, 45, 50, 53) sts along top right CO edge.

Begin Wave One
Rows 1-9: Work St st.

Note: Each size has its own section, cont with C1 held double.

Neck Shaping—Size 33.5" Only
Wave Inc Row (RS): K4, work Wave Pattern Row 1 over next 17 sts, K3, M1L, K1. 26 sts.
Work Wave Pattern Row 2.
Inc Row (RS): P to last st, M1L-P, K1. 27 sts. Break one strand C1.

Wave Two
Work with one strand C1 and one strand C2 held tog.
Setup Row (WS): P across.
Inc Row (RS): K to last st, M1L, K1. 1 st inc.
Next Row: P across.
Rep these two rows three more times. 31 sts.
Wave Inc Row (RS): K4, work Wave Pattern Row 1 over next 17 sts, (K2tog) two times, (YO, K1) two times, YO, K3. 32 sts.
Work Wave Pattern Row 2.
Next Inc Row (RS): P to last st, M1L-P, K1. 33 sts. Break C1.

Wave Three
Work with C2 held double.
Setup Row (WS): P across.
Inc Row (RS): K to last st, M1L, K1. 34 sts.
Next Row: P across.
CO Row: K across, CO 8 sts. 42 sts.
WE in St st for five rows.
Wave Row (RS): K4, work Wave Pattern Row 1 to last 4 sts, K4.
Work Wave Pattern Rows 2-3. Break one strand C2.

Wave Four

Work with one strand C2 and one strand MC held tog.

Rows 1-9: Work St st.

Wave Row (RS): K4, work Wave Pattern Row 1 to last 4 sts, K4. Work Wave Pattern Rows 2-3. Break C2.

Neck Shaping—Size 38" Only

Wave Inc Row (RS): K3, YO, K2, SSK, work Wave Pattern Row 1 over next 17 sts, K2tog, K2, YO, K1, YO, K2. 32 sts. Work Wave Pattern Row 2.

Inc Row (RS): P to last st, M1L-P, K1. 33 sts. Break one strand C1.

Wave Two

Work with one strand C1 and one strand C2 held tog.

Setup Row (WS): P across.

Inc Row (RS): K to last st, M1L, K1. 1 st inc.

Next Row: P across.

Rep these two rows three more times. 37 sts.

Wave Inc Row (RS): K3, YO, K2, SSK, work Wave Pattern Row 1 over next 17 sts, (K2tog) three times, (YO, K1) three times, YO, K4. 38 sts. Work Wave Pattern Row 2.

Next Inc Row (RS): P to last st, M1L-P, K1. 39 sts. Break C1.

Wave Three

Work with two strands C2 held tog.

Setup Row (WS): P across.

Inc Row (RS): K to last st, M1L, K1. 1 st inc.

Next Row: P across.

Rep these two rows once more. 41 sts.

CO Row (RS): K across, CO 7 sts. 48 sts.

WE in St st for three rows.

Next Row (RS): K3, YO, K2, SSK, work Wave Pattern Row 1 to last 7 sts, K2tog, K2, YO, K3. Work Wave Pattern Rows 2-3. Break one strand C2.

Wave Four

Work with one strand C2 and one strand MC held tog.

Rows 1-9: Work St st.

Next Row (RS): K3, YO, K2, SSK, work Wave Pattern Row 1 to last 7 sts, K2tog, K2, YO, K3. Work Wave Pattern Rows 2-3. Break C2.

Neck Shaping—Size 42.5" Only

Wave Inc Row (RS): K1, work Wave Pattern Row 1 over next 34 sts, M1L, K1. 37 sts. Work Row of 2 Wave Pattern.

Inc Row (RS): P to last st, M1L-P, K1. 38 sts. Break one strand C1.

Wave Two

Work with one strand C1 and one strand C2 held tog.

Setup Row (WS): P across.

Inc Row (RS): K to last st, M1L, K1. 1 st inc.

Next Row: P across.

Rep these two rows three more times. 42 sts.

Wave Inc Row (RS): K1, work Wave Pattern Row 1 over next 34 sts, K2tog, K2, YO, K1, YO, K2. 43 sts. Work Wave Pattern Row 2.

Next Inc Row (RS): P to last st, M1L-P, K1. 44 sts. Break C1.

Wave Three

Work with two strands C2 held tog.

Setup Row (WS): P across.

Inc Row (RS): K to last st, M1L, K1. 1 st inc.

Next Row: P across.

Rep these two rows two more times. 47 sts.

CO Row (RS): K across, CO 6 sts. 53 sts.

Next Row (WS): P across.

Wave Row: K1, work Wave Pattern Row 1 to last st, K1. Work Wave Pattern Rows 2-3. Break one strand C2.

Wave Four

Work with one strand C2 and one strand MC held tog.

Rows 1-9: Work St st.

Next Row (RS): K1, work Wave Pattern Row 1 to last st, K1. Work Wave Pattern Rows 2-3. Break C2.

Neck Shaping—Size 45.75" Only

Wave Row (RS): K4, work Wave Pattern Row 1 over next 34 sts, K1. Work Wave Pattern Row 2.

Inc Row (RS): P to last st, M1L-P, K1. 40 sts. Break one strand C1.

Wave Two

Work with one strand C1 and one strand C2 held tog.

Setup Row (WS): P across.

Inc Row (RS): K to last st, M1L, K1. 1 st inc.

Next Row: P across.

Rep these two rows three more times. 44 sts.

Wave Inc Row (RS): K4, work Wave Pattern Row 1 over next 34 sts, K3, YO, K3. 45 sts. Work Wave Pattern Row 2.

Next Inc Row (RS): P to last st, M1L-P, K1. 46 sts. Break C1.

Wave Three

Work with two strands C2 held tog.

Setup Row (WS): P across.

Inc Row (RS): K to last st, M1L, K1. 1 st inc.

Next Row: P across.

Rep these two rows three more times. 50 sts.

Wave CO Row (RS): K4, work Wave Pattern Row 1 to last 12 sts, (K2tog) three times, (YO, K1) two times, YO, K4, CO 9 sts. 59 sts. Work Wave Pattern Rows 2-3. Break one strand C2.

Wave Four

Work with one strand C2 and one strand MC held tog.

Rows 1-9: Work St st.

Wave Row (RS): K4, work Wave Pattern Row 1 to last 4 sts, K4. Work Wave Pattern Rows 2-3. Break C2.

Neck Shaping—Size 49.5" Only

Wave Row (RS): K6, work Wave Pattern Row 1 over next 34 sts, K5. Work Wave Pattern Row 2.

Inc Row (RS): P to last st, M1L-P, K1. 46 sts. Break one strand C1.

Wave Two

Work with one strand C1 and one strand C2 held tog.

Setup Row (WS): P across.

Inc Row (RS): K to last st, M1L, K1. 1 st inc.

Next Row: P across.

Rep these two rows three more times. 50 sts.

Wave Inc Row (RS): K6, work Wave Pattern Row 1 over next 34 sts, (K2tog) two times, (K1, YO) three times, K3. 51 sts. Work Wave Pattern Row 2.

Next Inc Row (RS): P to last st, M1L-P, K1. 52 sts. Break C1.

Wave Three

Work with two strands C2 held tog.

Setup Row (WS): P across.

Inc Row (RS): K to last st, M1L, K1. 1 st inc.

Next Row: P across.

Rep these two rows three more times. 56 sts.

Wave CO Row (RS): K6, work Wave Pattern Row 1 to last 16 sts, (K2tog) three times, (YO, K1) four times, YO, K2, (SSK) two times, CO 7 sts. 63 sts.

Work Wave Pattern Rows 2-3. Break one strand C2.

Wave Four

Work with one strand C2 and one strand MC held tog.

Rows 1-9: Work St st.

Wave Row (RS): K6, work Wave Pattern Row 1 to last 6 sts, K6. Work Wave Pattern Rows 2-3. Break C2.

Neck Shaping—Sizes 54" (58.25") Only

Wave Row (RS): K1 (4), work Wave Pattern Row 1 over next 34 sts, (K2tog) three times, (YO, K1) three times, YO, K3, SSK, K1. Work Wave Pattern Row 2.

Inc Row (RS): P to last st, M1L-P, K1. 51 (54) sts. Break one strand C1.

Wave Two

Work with one strand C1 and one strand C2 held tog.

Setup Row (WS): P across.

Inc Row (RS): K to last st, M1L, K1. 1 st inc.

Next Row: P across.

Rep these two rows three more times. 55 (58) sts.

Wave Inc Row (RS): K1 (4), work Wave Pattern Row 1 to last 3 sts, K2, M1L, K1. 56 (59) sts. Work Wave Pattern Row 2.

Next Inc Row (RS): P to last st, M1L-P, K1. 57 (60) sts. Break C1.

Wave Three

Work with two strands C2 held tog.

Setup Row (WS): P across.

Inc Row (RS): K to last st, M1L, K1. 1 st inc.

Next Row: P across.

Rep these two rows three more times. 61 (64) sts.

Wave Inc Row (RS): K1 (4), work Wave Pattern Row 1 to last 8 sts, (K2tog) two times, (YO, K1) two times, YO, K2. 62 (65) sts. Work Wave Pattern Row 2.

CO Row (RS): P across, CO 8 (11) sts. 70 (76) sts. Break one strand C2.

Wave Four

Work with one strand C2 and one strand MC held tog.

Rows 1-9: Work St st.

Wave Row (RS): K4, work Wave Pattern Row 1 to last 4 sts, K4. Work Wave Pattern Rows 2-3. Break C2.

Resume All Sizes

With MC held double, WE in St st until piece measures 7.5 (8, 8.5, 9, 9.25, 9.75, 9.75)", even with Back, ending on a WS row.

Place sts on st holder or scrap yarn. Break yarn.

Left Front

With RS facing, larger circular needles and C1 held double, PU and K 25 (31, 36, 39, 45, 50, 53) sts along top left CO edge.

Begin Wave One

Rows 1-9: Work St st.

Note: Each size has its own section, cont with C1 held double.

Neck Shaping—Size 33.5" Only

Wave Inc Row (RS): K1, M1R, K3, work Wave Pattern Row 1 over next 17 sts, K4. 26 sts.

Work Wave Pattern Row 2.

Inc Row (RS): K1, M1R-P, P to end. 27 sts. Break one strand C1.

Wave Two

Work with one strand C1 and one strand C2 held tog.

Setup Row (WS): P across.

Inc Row (RS): K1, M1R, K to end. 1 st inc.

Next Row: P across.

Rep these two rows three more times. 31 sts.

Wave Inc Row (RS): K3, (YO, K1) three times, (SSK) two times, work Wave Pattern Row 1 over next 17 sts, K4. 32 sts. Work Wave Pattern Row 2.

Next Inc Row (RS): K1, M1R-P, P to end. 33 sts. Break C1.

Wave Three

Work with two strands C2 held tog.

Setup Row (WS): P across.

Inc Row (RS): K1, M1R, K to end. 34 sts.

WE in St st for two rows.

CO Row (WS): P across, CO 8 sts. 42 sts.

WE in St st for four rows.

Next Row (RS): K4, work Wave Pattern Row 1 to last 4 sts, K4. Work Wave Pattern Rows 2-3. Break one strand C2.

Wave Four

With one strand C2 and one strand MC held tog, work same as Wave Four Right Front. Break C2.

Neck Shaping—Size 38" Only

Wave Inc Row (RS): K2, YO, K1, YO, K2, SSK, work Wave Pattern Row 1 over next 17 sts, K2tog, K2, YO, K3. 32 sts. Work Wave Pattern Row 2.

Inc Row (RS): K1, M1R-P, P to end. 33 sts. Break one strand C1.

Wave Two

Work with one strand C1 and one strand C2 held tog.

Setup Row (WS): P across.

Inc Row (RS): K1, M1R, K to end. 1 st inc.

Next Row: P across.

Rep these two rows three more times. 37 sts.

Wave Inc Row (RS): K4, (YO, K1) three times, YO, (SSK) three times, work Wave Pattern Row 1 over next 17 sts, K2tog, K2, YO, K3. 38 sts.
Work Wave Pattern Row 2.
Next Inc Row (RS): K1, M1R-P, P to end. 39 sts. Break C1.

Wave Three

Work with two strands C2 held tog.
Setup Row (WS): P across.
Inc Row (RS): K1, M1R, K to end. 1 st inc.
Next Row: P across.
Rep these two rows once more. 41 sts.
Next Row (RS): K across.
CO Row (WS): P across, CO 7 sts. 48 sts.
WE in St st for two rows.
Wave Row (RS): K3, YO, K2, SSK, work Wave Pattern Row 1 to last 7 sts, K2tog, K2, YO, K3.
Work Wave Pattern Rows 2-3. Break one strand C2.

Wave Four

With one strand C2 and one strand MC held tog, work same as Wave Four Right Front. Break C2.

Neck Shaping—Size 42.5" Only

Wave Inc Row (RS): K1, M1R, work Wave Pattern Row 1 over next 34 sts, K1. 37 sts.
Work Row of 2 Wave Pattern.
Inc Row (RS): K1, M1R-P, P to end. 38 sts. Break one strand C1.

Wave Two

Work with one strand C1 and one strand C2 held tog.
Setup Row (WS): P across.
Inc Row (RS): K1, M1R, K to end. 1 st inc.
Next Row: P across.
Rep these two rows three more times. 42 sts.
Wave Inc Row (RS): K1, work Wave Pattern Row 1 over next 34 sts, K2tog, K2, YO, K1, YO, K2. 43 sts.
Work Wave Pattern Row 2.
Next Inc Row (RS): K1, M1R-P, P to end. 44 sts. Break C1.

Wave Three

Work with two strands C2 held tog.
Setup Row (WS): P across.
Inc Row (RS): K1, M1R, K to end. 1 st inc.
Next Row: P across.
Rep these two rows two more times. 47 sts.
Next Row (RS): K across.
CO Row (WS): P across, CO 6 sts. 53 sts.
Wave Row: K1, work Wave Pattern Row 1 to last st, K1.
Work Wave Pattern Rows 2-3. Break one strand C2.

Wave Four

With one strand C2 and one strand MC held tog, work same as Wave Four Right Front. Break C2.

Neck Shaping—Size 45.75" Only

Wave Row (RS): K1, work Wave Pattern Row 1 over next 34 sts, K4.
Work Wave Pattern Row 2.
Inc Row (RS): K1, M1R-P, P to end. 40 sts. Break one strand C1.

Wave Two

Work with one strand C1 and one strand C2 held tog.
Setup Row (WS): P across.
Inc Row (RS): K1, M1R, K to end. 1 st inc.
Next Row: P across.
Rep these two rows three more times. 44 sts.
Wave Inc Row (RS): K3, YO, K3, work Wave Pattern Row 1 over next 34 sts, K4. 45 sts.
Work Wave Pattern Row 2.
Next Inc Row (RS): K1, M1R-P, P to end. 46 sts. Break C1.

Wave Three

Work with two strands C2 held tog.
Setup Row (WS): P across.
Inc Row (RS): K1, M1R, K to end. 1 st inc.
Next Row: P across.
Rep these two rows three more times. 50 sts.
Wave Row (RS): K4, (YO, K1) two times, YO, (SSK) three times, work Wave Pattern Row 1 to last 4 sts, K4.
CO Row (WS): P across, CO 9 sts. 59 sts.
Work Wave Pattern Row 3. Break one strand C2.

Wave Four

With one strand C2 and one strand MC held tog, work same as Wave Four Right Front. Break C2.

Neck Shaping—Size 49.5" Only

Wave Row (RS): K5, work Wave Pattern Row 1 over next 34 sts, K6.
Work Wave Pattern Row 2.
Inc Row (RS): K1, M1R-P, P to end. 46 sts. Break one strand C1.

Wave Two

Work with one strand C1 and one strand C2 held tog.
Setup Row (WS): P across.
Inc Row (RS): K1, M1R, K to end. 1 st inc.
Next Row: P across.
Rep these two rows three more times. 50 sts.
Wave Inc Row (RS): K3, (YO, K1) three times, (SSK) two times, work Wave Pattern Row 1 over next 34 sts, K6. 51 sts.
Work Wave Pattern Row 2.
Next Inc Row (RS): K1, M1R-P, P to end. 52 sts. Break C1.

Wave Three

Work with two strands C2 held tog.
Setup Row (WS): P across.
Inc Row (RS): K1, M1R, K to end. 1 st inc.
Next Row: P across.
Rep these two rows three more times. 56 sts.
Wave Row (RS): K1, K2tog, K4, (YO, K1) three times, YO, (SSK) three times, work Wave Pattern Row 1 to last 6 sts, K6.
CO Row (WS): P across, CO 7 sts. 63 sts.
Work Wave Pattern Row 3. Break one strand C2.

Wave Four

With one strand C2 and one strand MC held tog, work same as Wave Four Right Front. Break C2.

Neck Shaping—Sizes 54" (58.25") Only
Wave Row (RS): K1, SSK, K3, (YO, K1) three times, YO, (K2tog) three times, work Wave Pattern Row 1 over next 34 sts, K1 (4).
Work Wave Pattern Row 2.
Inc Row (RS): K1, M1R-P, P to end. 51 (54) sts. Break one strand C1.

Wave Two
Work with one strand C1 and one strand C2 held tog.
Setup Row (WS): P across.
Inc Row (RS): K1, M1R, K to end. 1 st inc.
Next Row: P across.
Rep these two rows three more times. 55 (58) sts.
Wave Inc Row (RS): K1, M1R, K2, work Wave Pattern Row 1 to last 1 (4) st(s), K1 (4). 56 (59) sts.
Work Wave Pattern Row 2.
Next Inc Row (RS): K1, M1R-P, P to end. 57 (60) sts. Break C1.

Wave Three
Work with two strands C2 held tog.
Setup Row (WS): P across.
Inc Row (RS): K1, M1R, K to end. 1 st inc.
Next Row: P across.
Rep these two rows three more times. 61 (64) sts.
Wave Inc Row (RS): K2, (YO, K1) three times, (K2tog) two times, work Wave Pattern Row 1 to last 1 (4) st(s), K1 (4). 62 (65) sts.
CO Row (WS): P across, CO 8 (11) sts. 70 (76) sts.
Work Wave Pattern Row 3. Break one strand C2.

Wave Four
With one strand C2 and one strand MC held tog, work same as Wave Four Right Front. Break C2.

Resume All Sizes
With MC held double, WE in St st until piece measures 7.5 (8, 8.5, 9, 9.25, 9.75, 9.75)", even with Back, ending on a WS row.

Body
Join Fronts and Back
Place held Back and Right Front sts on working needle. With MC held double and RS facing, K across Left Front, Back and Right Front. 177 (202, 227, 245, 266, 290, 313) sts.

WE in St st until piece measures 14" from underarm.
Sizes 33.5 (-, 42.5, 45.75, -, -, 58.25)" end on a WS row, sizes - (38, -, -, 49.5, 54, -)" end on a RS row.

Sizes - (38, -, -, 49.5, 54, -)" Only
Next Row (WS): P1, M1R-P, P to end. - (203, -, -, 267, 291, -) sts.

Hem (resume all sizes)
With smaller circular needles and MC held double, WE in 1x1 Rib for 3".
BO loosely in Rib.

Sleeves (make two the same)
With larger needles for working in the rnd and MC held double, PU and K 74 (80, 86, 90, 94, 100, 104) sts evenly around armhole, PM, and join for working in the rnd.

Initial Shaping—Sizes 33.5 (38, 42.5, 45.75, -, -, -)" Only
Dec Rnd: K1, K2tog, K to 3 sts before M, SSK, K1, SM. 2 sts dec; 72 (78, 84, 88) sts.
Next Rnd: K all.
Rep these two rnds 3 (3, 2, 1, -, -, -) more times. 6 (6, 4, 2, -, -, -) sts dec; 66 (72, 80, 86, -, -, -) sts.

Resume All Sizes
WE in St st until Sleeve measures 8 (7.25, 7.25, 7.25, 7.25, 7.25, 7.25)" from underarm.

Sleeve Shaping
Dec Rnd: K1, K2tog, K to 3 sts before M, SSK, K1, SM. 2 sts dec. Work St st and rep Dec Rnd every sixth rnd 10 (10, 4, 2, 0, 0, 0) more times, every fourth rnd 1 (3, 12, 15, 17, 13, 13) times, and then every other rnd 0 (0, 0, 0, 3, 10, 12) times. 22 (26, 32, 34, 40, 46, 50) sts dec; 42 (44, 46, 50, 52, 52, 52) sts. WE in St st until Sleeve measures 17.5 (18, 18, 18, 18, 18, 18.75)" from underarm.

Cuff
With smaller circular needles for working in the rnd and MC held double, WE in 1x1 Rib for 3".
BO loosely in Rib.

Collar & Button Bands
Collar
With smaller circular needles and MC held double, PU and K 97 (99, 105, 113, 111, 115, 127) sts along neck edge.
Row 1 (WS): (P1, K1) to last st, P1.
Row 2 (RS): (K1, P1) to last st, K1.
Rep Rows 1-2 until Collar measures 1.25".
BO loosely in Rib.

Buttonhole Band
With smaller circular needles, RS facing, and MC held double, PU and K 111 (113, 113, 115, 115, 117, 117) sts along Right Front.
Row 1 (WS): Sl1, (K1, P1) to end.
Row 2 (RS): Sl1, (P1, K1) to end.
Rep Rows 1-2 until Band measures 0.75", ending on a WS row.
Buttonhole Row 1 (RS): Work 5 (6, 6, 7, 7, 8, 8) sts in Rib as established, *BO 3 sts, work 11 sts in Rib; rep from * to last 8 (9, 9, 10, 10, 11, 11) sts, BO 3 sts, work 5 (6, 6, 7, 7, 8, 8) sts in Rib.
Buttonhole Row 2 (WS): Work in Rib to Buttonhole, (CO 3 sts, work 11 sts in Rib) to last Buttonhole, CO 3 sts, work to end in Rib.
WE in Rib as established until Band measures 1.25".
BO loosely in Rib.

Button Band
With smaller circular needles, RS facing, and MC held double, PU and K 111 (113, 113, 115, 115, 117, 117) sts along Left Front.
Row 1 (WS): Sl1, (K1, P1) to end.
Row 2 (RS): Sl1, (P1, K1) to end.
Rep Rows 1-2 until Band measures 1.25".
BO loosely in Rib.

Finishing
Weave in ends, wash, and block to diagram.
Sew on buttons opposite buttonholes.

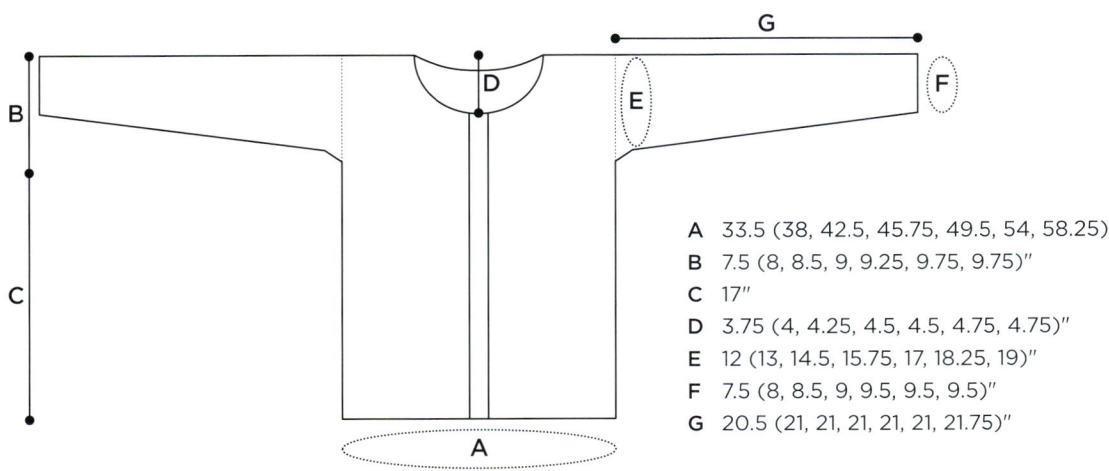

A 33.5 (38, 42.5, 45.75, 49.5, 54, 58.25)"
B 7.5 (8, 8.5, 9, 9.25, 9.75, 9.75)"
C 17"
D 3.75 (4, 4.25, 4.5, 4.5, 4.75, 4.75)"
E 12 (13, 14.5, 15.75, 17, 18.25, 19)"
F 7.5 (8, 8.5, 9, 9.5, 9.5, 9.5)"
G 20.5 (21, 21, 21, 21, 21, 21.75)"

PINECONE LACE HAT

by Emily Kintigh

FINISHED MEASUREMENTS
16 (19.25, 22.5)" circumference; meant
to be worn with approximately 2"
negative ease

YARN
Knit Picks Alpaca Cloud™ (fingering
weight, 100% Superfine Alpaca; 200
yards/50g): Anna 26877, 1 hank

NEEDLES
US 3 (3.25mm) 16" circular needles
and DPNs, or size to obtain gauge
US 1 (2.25mm) 16" circular needles,
or two sizes smaller than size used
to obtain gauge

NOTIONS
Yarn Needle
Stitch Markers

GAUGE
30 sts and 36 rnds = 4" in Pinecone
Lace Pattern in the round on larger
needles, blocked

For pattern support, contact auntieemsstudio@gmail.com

Pinecone Lace Hat

Notes:

This beautiful hat features a lovely lace pattern that resembles the shapes on the texture of a pinecone.
It is a wonderful way to show off a skein of luxury yarn.

The Pinecone Lace Hat is worked in the round from the brim up. The brim is 1x1 Twisted Rib. The lace patterning and crown decreases are both worked from charts.

The lace fabric has quite a bit of stretch and expands with blocking.

The chart is worked in the round; read each row from right to left as a RS row.

1x1 Twisted Rib (in the round over an even number of sts)
All Rnds: (K1 TBL, P1) to end.

DIRECTIONS

Brim
Loosely CO 120 (144, 168) sts onto smaller needles. PM and join in the rnd being careful not to twist sts.
Work 1x1 Twisted Rib until piece measures 1 (1.25, 1.5)" from CO edge.

Body
Switch to larger needles and begin working from Pinecone Lace chart; rep chart 10 (12, 14) times across each rnd.
Cont until piece measures approx 5 (5.5, 6)" from CO edge, ending with Rnd 8 of chart.

Crown
Work from Decrease Chart; rep chart 5 (6, 7) times across each rnd.
Break yarn and pull through remaining 5 (6, 7) sts.

Finishing
Weave in ends, wash, and block.

LEGEND

■	**No Stitch**	Placeholder—no stitch made
□	**Knit Stitch**	
○	**YO**	Yarn over
╱	**K2tog**	Knit 2 stitches together as one stitch
╲	**SSK**	Slip, slip, knit slipped stitches together
╱	**K3tog**	Knit 3 stitches together as one stitch
木	**SSSK**	(Slip 1 knit-wise) three times; insert left-hand needle from the front to the back of all stitches at the same time and knit them together
木	**SK2P**	Slip 1 knit-wise, K2tog, pass slip stitch over K2tog

Pinecone Lace

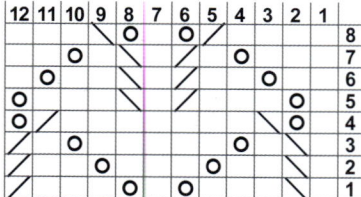

Decrease Chart

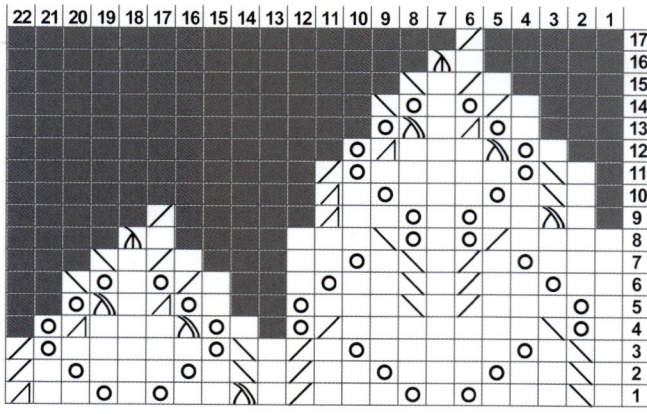

SIMPLEST MOHAIR PULLOVER

by Ann Weaver

FINISHED MEASUREMENTS

34 (38, 42, 46, 50, 54)" finished bust circumference; meant to be worn with approximately 2" positive ease

YARN

Knit Picks Aloft™ (lace weight, 72% Super Kid Mohair, 28% Silk; 260 yards/25g): C1 White 25213, C2 Pennyroyal 25206, 5 (5, 6, 7, 7, 9) balls each

NEEDLES

US 7 (4.5mm) 16" and 24" or longer circular needles, and DPNs or two 24" circular needles for two circulars technique or 32" or longer circular needles for Magic Loop technique, or size to obtain gauge

US 6 (4mm) 16" circular needles, or one size smaller than size used to obtain gauge

NOTIONS

Yarn Needle
2 Stitch Markers of different colors

GAUGE

16 sts and 24 rnds = 4" in Stockinette Stitch in the round with yarn held double, blocked

For pattern support, contact weaverknits77@gmail.com

Simplest Mohair Pullover

Notes:

A wardrobe staple that's as easy to knit as it is to wear, the Simplest Mohair Pullover brings feather-light luxury to a classic, flattering shape.

The Simplest Mohair Pullover is worked in the round from the bottom up and uses short rows to shape the dipped back hem. The yarn is held double throughout the pattern. The sleeves are picked up and worked in the round from the armholes down. The only seams to sew are at the shoulders!

DIRECTIONS

Body

Holding both C1 and C2 tog, loosely CO 68 (76, 84, 92, 100, 108) sts, PM, CO 68 (76, 84, 92, 100, 108) sts, PM of second color for BOR. Join to work in the rnd, being careful not to twist sts. 136 (152, 168, 184, 200, 216) sts.
Work 2x2 Rib until piece measures 2″ from CO edge.

Shape Back Hem

Short Row 1 (RS): K to 4 sts before M, W&T.
Short Row 2 (WS): P to 4 sts before BOR M, W&T.
Short Row 3: K to 4 sts before last wrapped st, W&T.
Short Row 4: P to 4 sts before last wrapped st, W&T.
Short Rows 5-12: Rep Short Rows 3-4.
Short Row 13: K to end, working wraps tog with wrapped sts.

Resume working in the rnd; WE in St st until piece measures 5.5″ from Front CO edge.

Shape Waist

Next Rnd: (K2, SSK, K to 4 sts before M, K2tog, K2, SM) two times. 4 sts dec; 132 (148, 164, 180, 196, 212) sts.
WE for nine rnds.
Rep these ten rnds two more times. 124 (140, 156, 172, 188, 204) sts.

Next Rnd: (K2, M1R, K to 2 sts before M, M1L, K2, SM) two times. 4 sts inc; 128 (144, 160, 176, 192, 208) sts.
WE for nine rnds.
Rep these ten rnds two more times. 136 (152, 168, 184, 200, 216) sts.

WE in St st until piece measures 18 (18, 18.5, 18.5, 18.5, 18.5)″ from Front CO edge.
On last rnd, BO last 4 (4, 4, 5, 5, 6) sts.

Divide Front & Back

BO 4 (4, 4, 5, 5, 6) sts at beginning of next rnd, K to 4 (4, 4, 5, 5, 6) sts before M, BO next 8 (8, 8, 10, 10, 12) sts, K to end. Turn, working only Front sts flat; leave Back sts on needle unworked. 60 (68, 76, 82, 90, 96) sts each for Front and Back.

Front

Next Row (WS): P across.
Next Row (RS): BO 2 (2, 2, 2, 3, 3) sts, K to end.
Next Row: BO 2 (2, 2, 2, 3, 3) sts, P to end. 56 (64, 72, 78, 84, 90) sts.

Next Row (RS): K2, SSK, K to last 4 sts, K2tog, K2. 2 sts dec; 54 (62, 70, 76, 82, 88) sts.
WE in St st for 3 (3, 3, 3, 1, 1) rows.
Rep these 4 (4, 4, 4, 2, 2) rows 0 (2, 1, 3, 3, 3) more time(s). 54 (58, 68, 70, 76, 82) sts.

Cont to WE in St st until armholes measure 5.5 (5.75, 6.25, 6.75, 7.5, 8)″ from underarm, ending with a WS row.

Shape Neck

Row 1 (RS): K17 (18, 23, 23, 25, 26), BO 20 (22, 22, 24, 26, 30) sts, K to end. 17 (18, 23, 23, 25, 26) sts each shoulder.
Row 2 (WS): P to gap, join a second pair of balls of yarn, P to end.
Row 3: K to 3 sts before gap, K2tog, K1; with first balls of yarn K1, SSK, K to end. 1 st dec each edge of neck.
Row 4: P to gap; P to end.
Rep Rows 3-4 four more times. 12 (13, 18, 18, 20, 21) sts each shoulder.

Shape Shoulders

Row 1 (RS): BO 4 (4, 6, 6, 6, 7) sts, K to gap; K to end.
Row 2 (WS): BO 4 (4, 6, 6, 6, 7) sts, P to gap; P to end.
Row 3: BO 4 (4, 6, 6, 7, 7) sts, K to gap; K to end.
Row 4: BO 4 (4, 6, 6, 7, 7) sts, P to gap; P to end.
Row 5: BO remaining 4 (5, 6, 6, 7, 7) sts.

Back

Rejoin yarns to back sts with WS facing. 60 (68, 76, 82, 90, 96) sts.
Next Row (WS): P across.
Next Row (RS): BO 2 (2, 2, 2, 3, 3) sts, K to end.
Next Row: BO 2 (2, 2, 2, 3, 3) sts, P to end. 56 (64, 72, 78, 84, 90) sts.

Next Row (RS): K2, SSK, K to last 4 sts, K2tog, K2. 2 sts dec; 54 (62, 70, 76, 82, 88) sts.
WE for 3 (3, 3, 3, 2, 2) rows in St st.
Rep these 4 (4, 4, 4, 3, 3) rows 0 (2, 1, 3, 3, 3) more time(s). 54 (58, 68, 70, 76, 82) sts.

WE as established until armholes measure 7 (7.25, 7.75, 8.25, 9, 9.5)″ from underarm, ending with a WS row.

Shape Neck & Shoulders

Row 1 (RS): K15 (16, 21, 21, 23, 24), BO 24 (26, 26, 28, 30, 34) sts, K to end. 15 (16, 21, 21, 23, 24) sts each shoulder.
Row 2 (WS): P to gap; join a second pair of balls of yarn, P to end.
Row 3: BO 4 (4, 6, 6, 6, 7) sts, K to gap; BO 3, K to end.
Row 4: BO 4 (4, 6, 6, 6, 7) sts, P to gap; BO 3, P to end.
Row 5: BO 4 (4, 6, 6, 7, 7) sts, K to gap; K to end.
Row 6: BO 4 (4, 6, 6, 7, 7) sts, P to gap; P to end.
Row 7: BO remaining 4 (5, 6, 6, 7, 7) sts at each shoulder.
Using yarn needle, sew shoulder seams tog.

Sleeves (make two the same)

With RS facing, using shorter circular needles and C1 and C2 held tog, beginning at center of underarm PU and K 25 (26, 29, 30, 32, 35) sts evenly spaced along back underarm and back of armhole, PM (this is M-1), PU and K 25 (26, 29, 30, 32, 35) sts evenly spaced along front of armhole and front underarm, PM of second color (M-2) for BOR. 50 (52, 58, 60, 64, 70) sleeve sts.

Short Row 1 (RS): K to 8 (8, 8, 8, 10, 12) sts after M-1, W&T.
Short Row 2 (WS): P to 8 (8, 8, 8, 10, 12) sts after M-1, W&T.
Short Row 3: K to 1 st past wrapped st, knitting wrap tog with wrapped st, W&T.
Short Row 4: P to 1 st past wrapped st, purling wrap tog with wrapped st, W&T.
Rep Short Rows 3-4 until 4 (4, 4, 5, 5, 6) sts remain unworked on either side of M-2, ending with a WS row.
Next Row (RS): K all sleeve sts, working wraps tog with wrapped sts. Remove M-1.
Work St st in the rnd until sleeve measures 1.5″ from underarm.

Dec Rnd: K2, SSK, K to last 4 sts, K2tog, K2. 2 sts dec; 48 (50, 56, 58, 62, 68) sts.
WE for 6 (5, 3, 3, 3, 3) rnds.
Rep these 7 (6, 4, 4, 4, 4) rnds 6 (7, 10, 11, 13, 16) more times. 36 sts. Change from 16″ circular needles to DPNs, or preferred method of knitting in the rnd, when sts no longer fit comfortably on needle.
WE in St st until sleeve measures 16″ from underarm.

Cuff

Work 2x2 Rib for 2″.
BO loosely in pattern.

Collar Edging

With RS facing, using smaller circular needles and C1 and C2 held tog, beginning at right back shoulder PU and K 41 (43, 43, 45, 47, 51) sts evenly spaced across back neck and 51 (53, 53, 55, 57, 61) sts evenly spaced across front neck. 92 (96, 96, 100, 104, 112) sts.
Work 2x2 Rib for 1″.
BO loosely in pattern.

Finishing

Weave in ends, wash, and block to diagram.

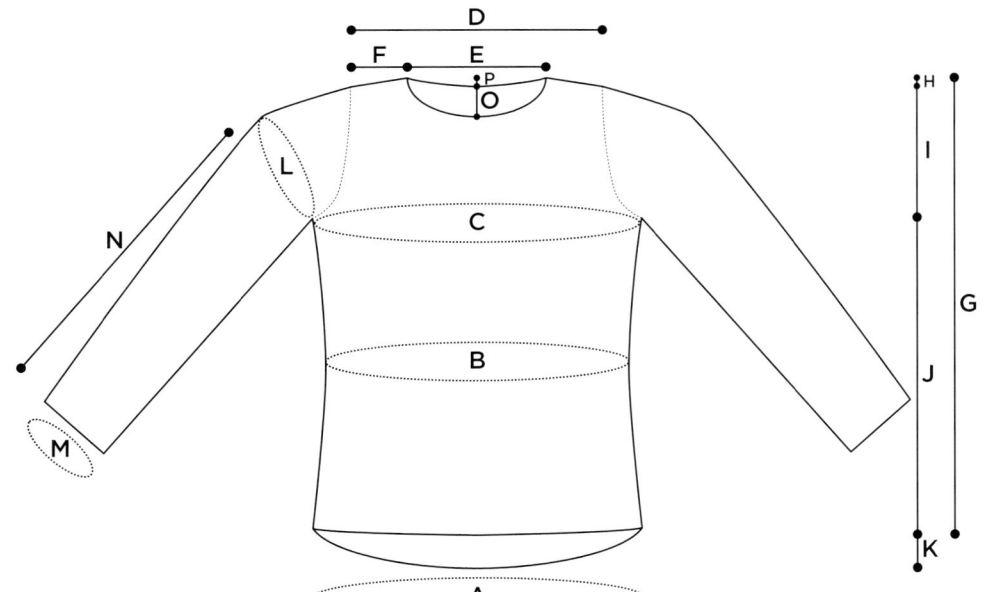

A	34 (38, 42, 46, 50, 54)″
B	31 (35, 39, 43, 47, 51)″
C	34 (38, 42, 46, 50, 54)″
D	13.5 (14.5, 17, 17.5, 19, 20.5)″
E	6.75 (8, 8, 8.5, 8.75, 10)″
F	3 (3.25, 4.5, 4.5, 5, 5.25)″
G	25.75 (26, 27, 27.5, 28.25, 28.75)″
H	0.5″
I	7.25 (7.5, 8, 8.5, 9.25, 9.75)″
J	18 (18, 18.5, 18.5, 18.5, 18.5)″
K	2″
L	12.5, (13, 14.5, 15, 16, 17.5)″
M	9″
N	18
O	1.75″
P	0.5″

SPLENDOR SCARF

by Amanda Wesley

FINISHED MEASUREMENTS

16" width × 70" length

YARN

Knit Picks Capretta™ Superwash
(fingering weight, 80% Fine Superwash
Merino Wool, 10% Cashmere, 10% Nylon;
230 yards/50g): Magnolia Heather 27641,
4 balls
Knit Picks Aloft™ (lace weight, 72% Super
Kid Mohair, 28% Silk; 260 yards/25g):
Blush 25205, 5 balls

NEEDLES

US 6 (4mm) straight or circular needles,
or size to obtain gauge

NOTIONS

Yarn Needle
Stitch Markers

GAUGE

24 sts and 32 rows = 4" in Lace Pattern
with one strand of each yarn held
together, blocked

For pattern support, contact amamarieknits@gmail.com

Splendor Scarf

Notes:

Combining Aloft's lustrous silk and mohair halo with the merino wool and brilliant cashmere in Capretta results in a piece that truly lives up to the shining splendor of its name.

The Splendor Scarf is a highly structural wide rectangular wrap, with columns of slipped stitches rising and falling along the length while a clean I-Cord edge frames the piece. Two strands of yarn are held together throughout; explore with color when combining fingering and lace weight yarns for this therapeutic knit.

Slip stitches purl-wise with yarn in back unless otherwise noted. When working Sl2 WYIF, make sure to keep float tension loose, otherwise the column of slipped stitches will be pinched.

I-Cord Cast On

CO 3 sts, slide sts to LH needle. (KFB, K2, slide 3 sts to LH needle) until there are 80 sts total. Slide 3 sts to LH needle, KFB, K2tog.

I-Cord Bind Off

CO 3 sts using Backward Loop Cast On onto beginning of row. (K2, SSK, slide 3 sts back to LH needle) until there are 3 sts remaining. BO 3 sts.

DIRECTIONS

Section 1

Using I-cord Cast On and one strand of each yarn held tog, CO 80 sts.

Setup Row (RS): Sl1, Sl1 WYIF, K1, P2, Sl2 WYIF, PM, P to last 3 sts, K1, Sl1 WYIF, P1.

Row 1 (WS): Sl1, K1, Sl1 WYIF, K to M, SM, (P2, K2) to last 3 sts, Sl1 WYIF, K1, P1.

Row 2: Sl1, Sl1 WYIF, K1, (P2, Sl2 WYIF) to M, SM, P to last 3 sts, K1, Sl1 WYIF, P1.

Rows 3-6: Rep Rows 1-2 twice.

Row 7: Rep Row 1.

Row 8, Column Inc (RS): Sl1, Sl1 WYIF, K1, (P2, Sl2 WYIF) to M, remove M, P2, Sl2 WYIF, PM, P to last 3 sts, K1, Sl1 WYIF, P1.

Work Rows 1-8 a total of 17 times, resulting in 18 Sl2 WYIF columns across piece. Remove M on final row.

Section 2

Row 1 (RS): Sl1, Sl1 WYIF, K1, (P2, Sl2 WYIF) to last 5 sts, P2, K1, Sl1 WYIF, P1.

Row 2 (WS): Sl1, K1, Sl1 WYIF, (K2, P2) to last 5 sts, K2, Sl1 WYIF, K1, P1.

Work Rows 1-2 a total of 150 times.

Work Row 1 once more.

Section 3

Setup Row (WS): Sl1, K1, Sl1 WYIF, K2, P2, K2, PM, (P2, K2) to last 3 sts, Sl1 WYIF, K1, P1.

Row 1 (RS): Sl1, Sl1 WYIF, K1, (P2, Sl2 WYIF) to M, SM, P to last 3 sts, K1, Sl1 WYIF, P1.

Row 2: Sl1, K1, Sl1 WYIF, K to M, SM, (P2, K2) to last 3 sts, Sl1 WYIF, K1, P1.

Rows 3-6: Rep Rows 1-2 twice.

Row 7: Rep Row 1.

Row 8, Column Dec (WS): Sl1, K1, Sl1 WYIF, K to M, remove M, P2, K2, PM (P2, K2) to last 3 sts, Sl1 WYIF, K1, P1.

Work Rows 1-8 a total of 16 times. Remove M on final row.

Row 9 (RS): Sl1, Sl1 WYIF, K1, P2, Sl2 WYIF, P to last 3 sts, K1, Sl1 WYIF, P1.

Row 10 (WS): Sl1, K1, Sl1 WYIF, K to last 7 sts, P2, K2, Sl1 WYIF, K1, P1.

Rep Rows 9-10 three more times.

BO using I-cord Bind Off.

Finishing

Weave in ends, wash, and block aggressively.

THEYA PULLOVER

by Kristen TenDyke

FINISHED MEASUREMENTS

33.5 (37.25, 42, 45.5, 50.5, 54, 58.75, 62.5, 67.25)″ finished bust circumference; meant to be worn with 1–2″ positive ease

YARN

Knit Picks Alpaca Cloud™ (lace weight, 100% Baby Alpaca; 440 yards/50g): Alfred 29798, Augusta 26796, 3 (3, 4, 4, 4, 5, 5, 5, 6) hanks each

NEEDLES

US 8 (5mm) DPNs and 32″ circular needles, or size to obtain gauge

US 7 (4.5mm) DPNs and 32″ circular needles, or one size smaller than size used to obtain gauge

NOTIONS

Yarn Needle
Stitch Markers
Scrap Yarn or Stitch Holders

GAUGE

20 sts and 26 rows = 4″ in Stockinette Stitch on larger needles worked flat and in the round with yarn held double, blocked

For pattern support, contact kristen@kristentendyke.com

Theya Pullover

Notes:

The soft halo of baby alpaca in lace weight creates a luxurious fabric knitted at a slightly loose gauge with two strands of yarn held together. Hold together two of the same color or use two different colors for a marled effect. The color possibilities are endless!

The Theya Pullover is worked seamlessly from the bottom up. The body is worked in the round, with short rows used to lengthen the back hemline. Sleeve stitches are picked up around the armhole edges. The cap is shaped with short rows, then the sleeve is worked in the round on DPNs to the cuff.

3x3 Rib (in the round over a multiple of 6 sts)
Rnd 1: (K3, P3) to end.
Rep Rnd 1 for pattern.

DIRECTIONS

Body

With smaller circular needles and one strand of each color held tog, CO 168 (186, 210, 228, 252, 270, 294, 312, 336) sts. PM for BOR and join to work in the rnd, being careful not to twist sts. BOR is at center of Back.
Work 3x3 Rib until piece measures 1.5" from CO edge. Change to larger circular needles.

Short Row Shaping

Short Row 1 (RS): K8 (9, 10, 12, 13, 14, 15, 17, 18), W&T.
Short Row 2 (WS): P8 (9, 10, 12, 13, 14, 15, 17, 18), SM, P8 (10, 11, 12, 13, 15, 16, 17, 18), W&T.
Cont working back and forth in rows as follows, slipping BOR M at center of each row.
Short Row 3 (RS): K to wrapped st from previous row, K wrap tog with st, K5 (5, 6, 6, 7, 7, 8, 8, 9), W&T.
Short Row 4 (WS): P to wrapped st from previous row, P wrap tog with st, P5 (5, 6, 6, 7, 7, 8, 8, 9), W&T.
Rep Short Rows 3-4 11 (11, 11, 12, 12, 12, 12, 13, 12) more times.
Next Row (RS): K to BOR M, SM, (K to wrapped st from previous row, K wrap tog with st) two times, K to end. Remove BOR M.

Shape Waist

Setup Rnd: K42 (46, 52, 57, 63, 67, 73, 78, 84), PM for new BOR, K84 (93, 105, 114, 126, 135, 147, 156, 168), PM for side, K to new BOR M. BOR is now at left side of Body.
Cont working St st, working waist shaping as follows.
Dec Rnd: (K1, K2tog, K to 3 sts before M, SSK, K1, SM) two times. 4 sts dec.
Rep Dec Rnd every twelve rnds 0 (0, 0, 0, 1, 1, 1, 2, 2) more times, then every ten rnds 4 (4, 4, 4, 3, 3, 3, 2, 2) times. 148 (166, 190, 208, 232, 250, 274, 292, 316) sts.
Work St st for nine rnds.

Inc Rnd: (K1, M1, K to 1 st before M, M1, K1, SM) two times. 4 sts inc.

Rep Inc Rnd every ten rnds 0 (0, 0, 0, 0, 2, 2, 3, 4) more times, then every eight rnds 4 (4, 4, 4, 4, 2, 2, 1, 0) times. 168 (186, 210, 228, 252, 270, 294, 312, 336) sts.
If necessary, cont to WE until Body measures 16 (16, 16.5, 16.5, 17, 17.5, 17.5, 18, 18.5)" from CO edge, measuring at center front to exclude short rows.

Divide Back & Front

Next Row (RS): *K to 5 (6, 7, 8, 9, 10, 11, 12, 13) sts before side M, BO next 10 (12, 14, 16, 18, 20, 22, 24, 26) sts, removing M; rep from * once more. 74 (81, 91, 98, 108, 115, 125, 132, 142) sts each Front and Back. Keep Back sts on circular needle or place them onto a st holder or scrap yarn to be worked later. Cont working back and forth on Front sts as follows.

Front

Shape Armholes

Armhole Dec Row (RS): K1, K2tog, K to last 3 sts, SSK, K1. 2 sts dec.
Next Row (WS): P across.
Rep the last two rows 2 (3, 5, 6, 8, 9, 11, 12, 14) more times. 68 (73, 79, 84, 90, 95, 101, 106, 112) sts.

Shape Neck

Next Row (RS): K1, K2tog, K27 (29, 32, 34, 37, 39, 42, 44, 47), join one more strand of each color held tog and BO next 8 (9, 9, 10, 10, 11, 11, 12, 12) sts, K27 (29, 32, 34, 37, 39, 42, 44, 47), SSK, K1. 29 (31, 34, 36, 39, 41, 44, 46, 49) sts remain on each side. Cont working both sides at the same time, with two separate strands of yarn for each Front.

Size 33.5" Only
Row 1 (WS): P to neck edge; on other side BO 5 sts, P to end. 29 sts on Left Front and 24 sts on Right Front.
Row 2 (RS): K to neck edge; on other side BO 5 sts, K to end. 24 sts on each side.

Sizes - (37.25, 42, 45.5, 50.5, 54, 58.75, 62.5, 67.25)" Only
Row 1 (WS): P to neck edge; on other side BO 5 sts, P to end. - (31, 34, 36, 39, 41, 44, 46, 49) sts on Left Front and - (26, 29, 31, 34, 36, 39, 41, 44) sts on Right Front.
Row 2 (RS): K1, K2tog, K to neck edge; on other side BO 5 sts, K to last 3 sts, SSK, K1. - (25, 28, 30, 33, 35, 38, 40, 43) sts on each side.

Sizes 33.5 (37.25, -, -, -, -, -, -, -)" Only
Row 3 (WS): P to neck edge; on other side BO 3 sts, P to end. 24 (25, -, -, -, -, -, -, -) sts on Left Front and 21 (22, -, -, -, -, -, -, -) sts on Right Front.
Row 4 (RS): K to neck edge; on other side BO 3 sts, K to end. 21 (22, -, -, -, -, -, -, -) sts on each side.

Sizes - (-, 42, 45.5, 50.5, 54, 58.75, 62.5, 67.25)" Only
Row 3 (WS): P to neck edge; on other side BO 3 sts, P to end. - (-, 28, 30, 33, 35, 38, 40, 43) sts on Left Front and - (-, 25, 27, 30, 32, 35, 37, 40) sts on Right Front.

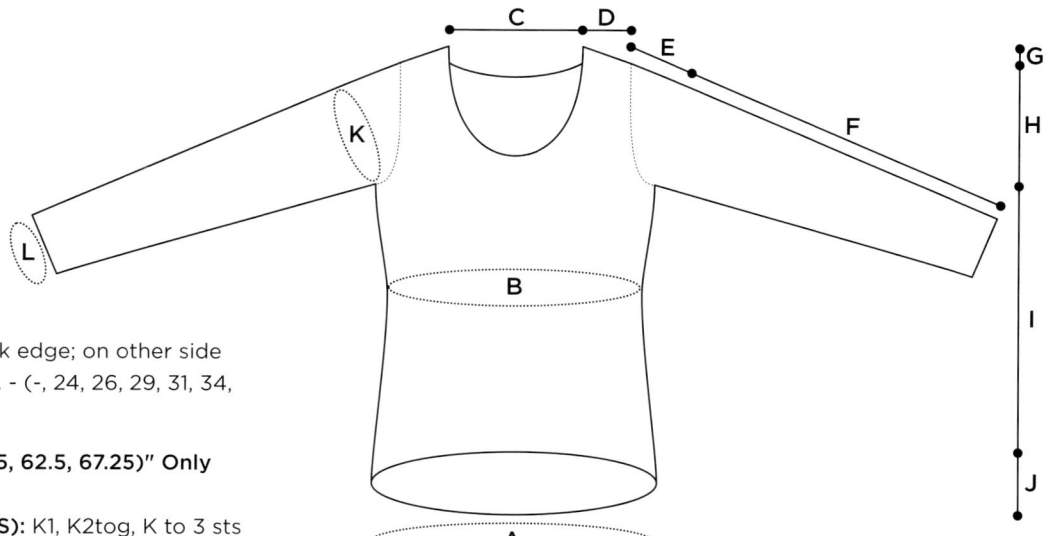

Row 4 (RS): K1, K2tog, K to neck edge; on other side BO 3 sts, K to last 3 sts, SSK, K1. - (-, 24, 26, 29, 31, 34, 36, 39) sts on each side.

Sizes - (-, -, 45.5, 50.5, 54, 58.75, 62.5, 67.25)″ Only
Next Row (WS): P across.
Neck and Armhole Dec Row (RS): K1, K2tog, K to 3 sts before neck edge, SSK, K1; on other side K1, K2tog, K to last 3 sts, SSK, K1. 2 sts dec on each Front.
Rep last two rows - (-, -, 0, 1, 2, 3, 4, 5) more times.
- (-, -, 24, 25, 25, 26, 26, 27) sts on each Front.

Resume All Sizes
Next Row (WS): P across.
Neck Dec Row (RS): K to 3 sts before neck edge, SSK, K1; on other side K1, K2tog, K to end. 1 st dec on each Front.
Rep last two rows 6 (6, 6, 5, 4, 3, 2, 1, 0) more times.
14 (15, 17, 18, 20, 21, 23, 24, 26) sts on each Front.
Cont to WE until armholes measure 7 (7.25, 7.75, 8.25, 8.75, 9.25, 9.75, 10, 10.5)″, ending after a WS row.

Shape Shoulders
Short Row 1 (RS): K to neck edge; on other side, K10 (11, 12, 13, 15, 15, 17, 18, 19), W&T.
Short Row 2 (WS): P to neck edge; on other side, P10 (11, 12, 13, 15, 15, 17, 18, 19), W&T.
Short Row 3: K to neck edge; on other side, K6 (7, 8, 8, 10, 10, 11, 12, 12), W&T.
Short Row 4: P to neck edge; on other side, P6 (7, 8, 8, 10, 10, 11, 12, 12), W&T.
Short Row 5: K to neck edge; on other side, K3 (3, 4, 4, 5, 5, 5, 6, 6), W&T.
Short Row 6: P to neck edge; on other side, P3 (3, 4, 4, 5, 5, 5, 6, 6), W&T.
Next Row (RS): K to neck edge; on other side, K to end working wraps tog with their sts as you pass them.
Next Row (WS): P to neck edge; on other side, P to end working wraps tog with their sts as you pass them.
Place all sts onto st holders or scrap yarn for shoulders. Break yarn.

Back
Return 74 (81, 91, 98, 108, 115, 125, 132, 142) held Back sts to larger needles and join one strand of each color held tog, preparing to work a RS row.

Shape Armholes
Armhole Dec Row (RS): K1, K2tog, K to last 3 sts, SSK, K1. 2 sts dec.
Next Row (WS): P across.

A	33.5 (37.25, 42, 45.5, 50.5, 54, 58.75, 62.5, 67.25)″
B	29.5 (33.25, 38, 41.5, 46.5, 50, 54.75, 58.5, 63.25)″
C	7.5 (7.75, 7.75, 8, 8, 8.25, 8.25, 8.5, 8.5)″
D	2.75 (3, 3.5, 3.5, 4, 4.25, 4.5, 4.75, 5.25)″
E	3.75 (4, 4.25, 4.5, 5, 5.25, 5.5, 5.75, 6.25)″
F	19.5 (20, 20, 20.5, 20.5, 21, 21, 21.5, 21.5)″
G	1″
H	7 (7.25, 7.75, 8.25, 8.75, 9.25, 9.75, 10, 10.5)″
I	16 (16, 16.5, 16.5, 17, 17.5, 17.5, 18, 18.5)″
J	3.75 (3.75, 3.75, 4, 4, 4, 4, 4.25, 4)″
K	13.25 (14.5, 15.5, 16.75, 18, 19.25, 20.5, 21.5, 22.75)″
L	8.5 (8.5, 9.5, 9.5, 10.75, 10.75, 10.75, 12, 12)″

Rep last two rows 3 (5, 8, 10, 13, 15, 18, 20, 23) more times. 66 (69, 73, 76, 80, 83, 87, 90, 94) sts.
WE in St st until armholes measure 5.25 (5.5, 6, 6.5, 7, 7.5, 8, 8.25, 8.75)″ from underarm BO sts, ending after a WS row.

Shape Neck
Next Row (RS): K19 (20, 22, 23, 25, 26, 28, 29, 31), join one more strand of each color held tog and BO next 28 (29, 29, 30, 30, 31, 31, 32, 32) sts, K to end. 19 (20, 22, 23, 25, 26, 28, 29, 31) sts each side. Cont working both sides at the same time, using two separate strands of yarn for each side.
Next Row (WS): P across.
Neck Dec Row (RS): K to 3 sts before neck edge, SSK, K1; on other side, K1, K2tog, K to end. 1 st dec each side.
Rep last two rows four more times. 14 (15, 17, 18, 20, 21, 23, 24, 26) sts each side for shoulders.
Next Row (WS): P across.

Shape Shoulders
Work same as for Front.

Join Shoulders
Return 14 (15, 17, 18, 20, 21, 23, 24, 26) held sts from each of the Front shoulders to DPNs and join them to the Back shoulders with 3-Needle Bind Off Method.

Sleeves

With RS facing, larger DPNs, and one strand of each color held tog, begin at center of underarm BO sts, PU and K 5 (6, 7, 8, 9, 10, 11, 12, 13) sts evenly along first half of underarm BO sts, PU and K 28 (30, 32, 34, 36, 38, 40, 42, 44) sts along armhole edge to top of shoulder, PM for shoulder, PU and K 28 (30, 32, 34, 36, 38, 40, 42, 44) sts evenly to remaining underarm BO sts, PU and K 5 (6, 7, 8, 9, 10, 11, 12, 13) sts in BO sts. 66 (72, 78, 84, 90, 96, 102, 108, 114) sts.

Shape Cap with Short Rows

Short Row 1 (RS): K to shoulder M, SM, K7, W&T.
Short Row 2 (WS): P to shoulder M, remove M, P7, W&T. 25 (28, 31, 34, 37, 40, 43, 46, 49) sts remain unworked at each end of row.
Short Row 3: K to wrapped st from previous row, K wrap tog with st, K1, W&T.
Short Row 4: P to wrapped st from previous row, P wrap tog with st, P1, W&T.
Rep Short Rows 3-4 8 (9, 10, 11, 12, 13, 14, 15, 16) more times. 7 (8, 9, 10, 11, 12, 13, 14, 15) sts remain unworked at each end of row.
Short Row 5 (RS): K to wrapped st from previous row, K wrap tog with st, W&T.
Short Row 6 (WS): P to wrapped st from previous row, P wrap tog with st, W&T.
Rep Short Rows 5-6 one more time. 5 (6, 7, 8, 9, 10, 11, 12, 13) sts remain unworked at each end of row.
Next Row (RS): K all, working wraps tog with their sts as they appear. Cont working in the rnd.

Shape Sleeve

Dec Rnd (RS): K1, K2tog, K to last 3 sts, SSK, K1. 2 sts dec. Work St st and rep Dec Rnd every 8 (6, 6, 6, 6, 4, 4, 4, 4) rnds 3 (2, 2, 12, 12, 1, 10, 9, 18) more times, then every 10 (8, 8, 8, 8, 6, 6, 6, 6) rnds 8 (12, 12, 5, 5, 19, 13, 14, 8) times. 42 (42, 48 48, 54, 54, 54, 60, 60) sts.
WE in St st until sleeve measures 18 (18.5, 18.5, 19, 19, 19.5, 19.5, 20, 20)" from underarm.
Change to smaller DPNs and work 3x3 Rib for 1.5".
BO all sts loosely in pattern.

Finishing

Neckband

With RS facing, smaller circular needles and one strand of each color held tog, begin at right shoulder seam, PU and K 12 (11, 11, 11, 11, 12, 12, 12, 12) sts along Right Back neckline to BO sts, PU and K 28 (29, 29, 30, 30, 31, 31, 32, 32) sts along Back BO sts, PU and K 12 (11, 11, 11, 11, 12, 12, 12, 12) sts along Left Back neckline to shoulder, PU and K 28 (28, 28, 27, 27, 28, 28, 27, 27) sts along Left Front neckline to BO sts, PU and K 24 (25, 25, 26, 26, 27, 27, 28, 28) sts along Front BO sts, PU and K 28 (28, 28, 27, 27, 28, 28, 27, 27) sts along Right Front neckline to shoulder. 132 (132, 132, 132, 132, 138, 138, 138, 138) sts. PM for BOR and join to work in the rnd. Work 3x3 Rib for 1.5".
BO all sts loosely in pattern.

Weave in ends, wash, and block to diagram.

TIMELESS PULLOVER

by Emily Ringelman

FINISHED MEASUREMENTS

30.5 (33.5, 36, 39, 42, 45.25, 48, 51.25, 54)" finished bust circumference; meant to be worn with 2-3" positive ease

YARN

Knit Picks Aloft™ (lace weight, 72% Super Kid Mohair, 28% Silk; 260 yards/25g): Carbon 25758, 5 (5, 6, 7, 8, 9, 10, 11, 12) balls

NEEDLES

US 6 (4mm) 16" and 24" circular needles and DPNs, or size to obtain gauge

NOTIONS

Yarn Needle
Stitch Markers
Scrap Yarn or Stitch Holder

GAUGE

20 sts and 28 rnds = 4" in Stockinette Stitch in the round with yarn held double, blocked

For pattern support, contact emily.ringelman@gmail.com

Timeless Pullover

Notes:

Evoking a trio of pearl necklaces, the bands on the yoke of this pullover make the increases part of the design. Fluffy Aloft, held double, brings a sense of luxury and timelessness to this otherwise simple pullover.

This circular-yoked pullover is worked from the top down in the round, with short rows to raise the back of the neck. Two raglan increase rounds worked just before the divide help curve the sweater into the underarm. Instructions are included for optional waist shaping. The yarn is held double throughout, and edgings are simple Garter Stitch.

DIRECTIONS

Yoke

With shorter circular needles and yarn held double, CO 95 (100, 100, 105, 105, 110, 110, 115, 115) sts. Join to work in the rnd, being careful not to twist sts. PM for BOR, which is center back.
Work Garter st in the rnd for 1".

Short Row 1 (RS): K12 (14, 15, 15, 16, 17, 17, 18, 18), W&T.
Short Row 2 (WS): P to BOR, SM, P12 (14, 15, 15, 16, 17, 17, 18, 18), W&T.
Short Row 3: K to BOR, SM, K15 (17, 18, 18, 19, 20, 20, 21, 21), W&T.
Short Row 4: P to BOR, SM, P15 (17, 18, 18, 19, 20, 20, 21, 21), W&T.
Short Row 5: K to BOR.
Knit one rnd, picking up and hiding wraps.

Yoke Increases

Next Rnd: Switching to longer circular needles as you work, *K0 (25, 9, 8, 15, 13, 7, 6, 4), M1; work from * a total of 0 (4, 11, 12, 7, 8, 15, 17, 27) times, K to end. 95 (104, 111, 117, 112, 118, 125, 132, 142) sts.
Work St st for 9 (10, 11, 11, 11, 12, 13, 14, 15) rnds.
Next Rnd: P all.
Yoke Inc Rnd 1: *K3 (3, 3, 3, 2, 2, 2, 2, 2), YO; rep from * to last 2 (2, 0, 0, 2, 2, 1, 0, 2) sts, K to end. 126 (138, 148, 156, 167, 176, 187, 198, 212) sts.
Next Rnd: P all.
Work St st for 9 (10, 11, 11, 11, 12, 13, 14, 15) rnds.
Next Rnd: P all.
Yoke Inc Rnd 2: (K3, YO) to last 0 (0, 1, 0, 2, 2, 1, 0, 2) sts, K to end. 168 (184, 197, 208, 222, 234, 249, 264, 282) sts.
Next Rnd: P all.
Work St st for 9 (10, 11, 11, 11, 12, 13, 14, 15) rnds.
Next Rnd: P all.
Yoke Inc Rnd 3: (K3, YO) to last 0 (1, 2, 1, 0, 0, 0, 0, 0) sts, K to end. 224 (245, 262, 277, 296, 312, 332, 352, 376) sts.
Next Rnd: P all.

Work St st until piece measures 6.75 (7, 7.25, 7.75, 7.75, 8.25, 8.5, 9.25, 9.75)" from CO edge in front.

Next Rnd: K32 (35, 39, 41, 45, 48, 52, 55, 58) back sts, PM, K48 (51, 53, 55, 57, 59, 62, 66, 71) sleeve sts, PM, K64 (72, 78, 84, 91, 97, 104, 110, 117) front sts, PM, K48 (51, 53, 55, 57, 59, 62, 66, 71) sleeve sts, PM, K32 (36, 39, 42, 46, 49, 52, 55, 59) back sts.
Raglan Inc Rnd: (K to 1 st before M, M1R, K1, SM, K1, M1L) four times, K to end. 8 sts inc.
Knit one rnd.
Rep Raglan Inc Rnd. 240 (261, 278, 293, 312, 328, 348, 368, 392) sts.
Knit one rnd. Yoke should measure 7.5 (7.75, 8, 8.5, 8.5, 9, 9.25, 10, 10.5)" from CO edge in front.

Divide Body & Sleeves

Next Rnd: K to M, remove M, place next 52 (55, 57, 59, 61, 63, 66, 70, 75) sleeve sts on scrap yarn or st holder, CO 8 (8, 8, 10, 10, 12, 12, 14, 14) sts, remove M and place it at center of newly CO sts for new BOR, K across front sts to next M, remove M, place next 52 (55, 57, 59, 61, 63, 66, 70, 75) sleeve sts on scrap yarn or st holder, CO 8 (8, 8, 10, 10, 12, 12, 14, 14) sts, remove M, K to end. 152 (167, 180, 195, 210, 226, 240, 256, 270) sts for Body.

Body

Waist Shaping

If you would like a more casual silhouette, cont to Body Without Waist Shaping, below.
WE in St st until piece measures 2 (2, 2.5, 2.5, 3, 3, 3.5, 3.5, 4)" from underarm, or, if you are able to try on the sweater, until 1" below bust apex.
Next Rnd: K19 (21, 23, 25, 26, 28, 30, 32, 34), PM for bust decs, K38 (41, 44, 47, 53, 57, 60, 64, 67), PM for bust decs, K to end.
Bust Dec Rnd: K to 3 sts before M, SSK, K1, SM, K to M, SM, K1, K2tog, K to end. 2 sts dec.
Work St st and rep Bust Dec Rnd every fourth rnd four more times. 142 (157, 170, 185, 200, 216, 230, 246, 260) sts.
WE in St st for 2 (2, 2, 2, 2.5, 2.5, 3, 3, 3)".
Hip Inc Rnd: K to 1 st before M, M1R, K1, SM, K to M, SM, K1, M1L, K to end. 2 sts inc.
Work St st and rep Hip Inc Rnd every fourth rnd eight more times. 160 (175, 188, 203, 218, 234, 248, 264, 278) sts.
WE in St st until Body measures 14.75 (14.75, 14.75, 15, 15.5, 16.25, 16.5, 16.5, 16.75)" from underarm CO, or to 2" shorter than desired length.
Work Garter st for 2".
BO all sts.

Without Waist Shaping

WE in St st until Body measures 14.75 (14.75, 14.75, 15, 15.5, 16.25, 16.5, 16.5, 16.75)" from underarm CO, or to 2" shorter than desired length.
Work Garter st for 2".
BO all sts.

Sleeves (make two the same)

Switch to DPNs when work becomes tight on circular needles.

Return held 52 (55, 57, 59, 61, 63, 66, 70, 75) sleeve sts to shorter circular needles.

Beginning at center of underarm CO, PU and K 4 (4, 4, 5, 5, 6, 6, 7, 7) sts in underarm CO, K across sleeve sts, PU and K 4 (4, 4, 5, 5, 6, 6, 7, 7) sts in underarm CO. Join to work in the rnd and PM for BOR. 60 (63, 65, 69, 71, 75, 78, 84, 89) sts. Knit four rnds.

Dec Rnd: K1, K2tog, K to 3 sts before M, SSK, K1. 2 sts dec. Work St st and rep Dec Rnd every 8 (8, 8, 7, 7, 6, 6, 5, 5) rnds 13 (14, 14, 16, 16, 18, 19, 22, 24) more times. 32 (33, 35, 35, 37, 37, 38, 38, 39) sts.

WE in St st until sleeve measures 19", or 2" shorter than desired length.
Work Garter st for 2".
BO all sts.

Finishing

Weave in ends, wash, and block to diagram.

A   30.5 (33.5, 36, 39, 42, 45.25, 48, 51.25, 54)"
B   28.5 (31.5, 34, 37, 40, 43.25, 46, 49.25, 52)" (optional waist shaping)
C   32 (35, 37.5, 40.5, 43.5, 46.75, 49.5, 52.75, 55.5)" (without waist shaping, C is the same as A)
D   12 (12.5, 13, 13.5, 14.25, 15, 15.5, 16.75, 17.75)"
E   6.5 (6.5, 7, 7, 7.5, 7.5, 7.5, 7.5, 7.75)"
F   16.75 (16.75, 16.75, 17, 17.5, 18.25, 18.5, 18.5, 18.75)"
G   9.5 (10, 10, 10.5, 10.5, 11, 11, 11.5, 11.5)"
H   21"
I   7.5 (7.75, 8, 8.5, 8.5, 9, 9.25, 10, 10.5)"

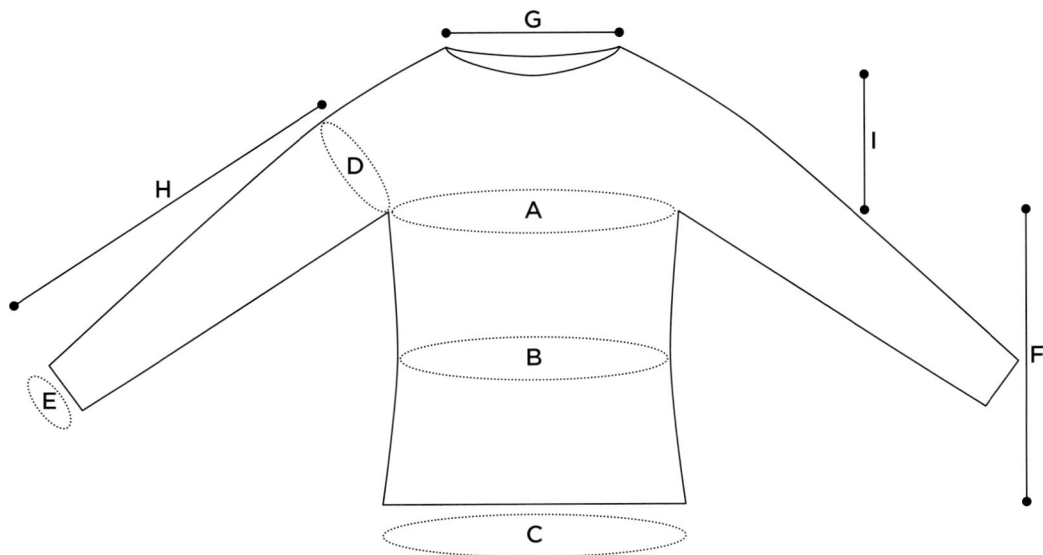

Glossary
Common Stitches & Techniques

Slipped Stitches (Sl)
Always slip stitches purl-wise with yarn held to the wrong side of work, unless noted otherwise in the pattern.

Make 1 Left-Leaning Stitch (M1L)
Inserting LH needle from front to back, PU the horizontal strand between the st just worked and the next st, and K TBL.

Make 1 Right-Leaning Stitch (M1R)
Inserting LH needle from back to front, PU the horizontal strand between the st just worked and the next st, and K TFL.

Slip, Slip, Knit (SSK)
(Sl1 K-wise) twice; insert LH needle into front of these 2 sts and knit them together.

Centered Double Decrease (CDD)
Slip first and second sts together as if to work K2tog; K1; pass 2 slipped sts over the knit st.

Stockinette Stitch (St st, flat over any number of sts)
Row 1 (RS): Knit all sts.
Row 2 (WS): Purl all sts.
Rep Rows 1-2 for pattern.
St st in the round: Knit every rnd.

Garter Stitch (in the round over any number of sts)
Rnd 1: Purl all sts.
Rnd 2: Knit all sts.
Rep Rnds 1-2 for pattern.
Garter Stitch flat: Knit every row.
(One Garter ridge is comprised of two rows/rnds.)

1x1 Rib (flat or in the round, over an even number of sts)
Row/Rnd 1: (K1, P1) to end of row/rnd.
Rep Row/Rnd 1 for pattern.

2x2 Rib (flat over a multiple of 4 sts plus 2)
Row 1 (RS): K2, (P2, K2) to end of row.
Row 2 (WS): P2, (K2, P2) to end of row.
Rep Rows 1-2 for pattern.

2x2 Rib (in the round over a multiple of 4 sts)
Rnd 1: (K2, P2) to end of rnd.
Rep Rnd 1 for pattern.

Magic Loop Technique
A technique using one long circular needle to knit in the round around a small circumference. A tutorial can be found at https://tutorials.knitpicks.com/wptutorials/magic-loop.

Knitting in the Round with Two Circular Needles
A technique using two long circulars to knit around a small circumference. A tutorial can be found at https://tutorials.knitpicks.com/knitting-in-the-round-with-2-circular-needles.

Backward Loop Cast On
A simple, all-purpose cast on that can be worked mid-row. Also called Loop, Single, or E-Wrap Cast On. A tutorial can be found at https://tutorials.knitpicks.com/loop-cast-on.

Long Tail Cast On
Fast and neat once you get the hang of it. Also referred to as the Slingshot Cast On. A tutorial can be found at https://tutorials.knitpicks.com/long-tail-cast-on.

Cabled Cast On
A strong and nice looking basic cast on that can be worked mid-project. A tutorial can be found at https://tutorials.knitpicks.com/cabled-cast-on.

3-Needle Bind Off
Used to easily seam two rows of live stitches together. A tutorial can be found at https://tutorials.knitpicks.com/3-needle-bind-off.

Abbreviations

approx	approximately	**KFB**	knit into front and back of stitch	**PSSO**	pass slipped stitch over	**SSP**	slip, slip, purl these 2 stitches together through back loop
BO	bind off						
BOR	beginning of round	**K-wise**	knit-wise	**PU**	pick up		
CN	cable needle	**LH**	left hand	**P-wise**	purl-wise	**SSSK**	slip, slip, slip, knit these 3 stitches together (like SSK)
C (1, 2...)	color (1, 2...)	**M**	marker	**rep**	repeat		
CC	contrast color	**M1**	make 1 stitch	**Rev St st**	reverse stockinette stitch		
CDD	centered double decrease (*see above*)	**M1L**	make 1 left-leaning stitch (*see above*)			**St st**	stockinette stitch (*see above*)
				RH	right hand		
CO	cast on	**M1R**	make 1 right-leaning stitch (*see above*)	**rnd(s)**	round(s)	**st(s)**	stitch(es)
cont	continue			**RS**	right side	**TBL**	through back loop
dec(s)	decrease(es)	**MC**	main color	**Sk**	skip	**TFL**	through front loop
DPN(s)	double pointed needle(s)	**P**	purl	**SK2P**	slip 1, knit 2 together, pass slipped stitch over	**tog**	together
		P2tog	purl 2 stitches together			**W&T**	wrap & turn (for short rows; *see next pg*)
inc(s)	increase(s)			**SKP**	slip, knit, pass slipped stitch over		
K	knit	**P3tog**	purl 3 stitches together			**WE**	work even
K2tog	knit 2 stitches together			**Sl**	slip (*see above*)	**WS**	wrong side
		PM	place marker	**SM**	slip marker	**WYIB**	with yarn in back
K3tog	knit 3 stitches together	**PFB**	purl into front and back of stitch	**SSK**	slip, slip, knit these 2 stitches together (*see above*)	**WYIF**	with yarn in front
						YO	yarn over

Cabling Without a Cable Needle
A tutorial can be found at https://tutorials.knitpicks.com /learn-to-cable-without-a-cable-needle.

Felted Join (to splice yarn)
One method for joining a new length of yarn to the end of one that is already being used. A tutorial can be found at https://tutorials.knitpicks.com/felted-join.

Mattress Stitch
A neat, invisible seaming method that uses the bars between the first and second stitches on the edges. A tutorial can be found at https://tutorials.knitpicks.com/mattress-stitch.

Provisional Cast On (crochet method)
Used to cast on stitches that are also a row of live stitches, so they can be put onto a needle and used later.
Directions: Using a crochet hook, make a slipknot, then hold knitting needle in left hand, hook in right. With yarn in back of needle, work a chain st by pulling yarn over needle and through chain st. Move yarn back to behind needle, and rep for the number of sts required. Chain a few more sts off the needle, then break yarn and pull end through last chain. (CO sts may be incorrectly mounted; if so, work into backs of these sts.) To unravel later (when sts need to be picked up), pull chain end out; chain should unravel, leaving live sts. A video tutorial can be found at https://tutorials.knitpicks .com/crocheted-provisional-cast-on.

Provisional Cast On (crochet chain method)
Same result as the crochet method above, but worked differently, so you may prefer one or the other.
Directions: With a crochet hook, use scrap yarn to make a slipknot and chain the number of sts to be cast on, plus a few extra sts. Insert tip of knitting needle into first bump of crochet chain. Wrap project yarn around needle as if to knit, and pull yarn through crochet chain, forming first st. Rep this process until you have cast on the correct number of sts. To unravel later (when sts need to be picked up), pull chain out, leaving live sts. A photo tutorial can be found at https:// tutorials.knitpicks.com/crocheted-provisional-cast-on.

Judy's Magic Cast On
This method creates stitches coming out in opposite directions from a seamless center line, perfect for starting toe-up socks.
Directions: Make a slipknot and place loop around one of the two needles; anchor loop counts as first st. Hold needles tog, with needle that yarn is attached to on top. In other hand, hold yarn so tail goes over index finger and yarn attached to ball goes over thumb. Bring tip of bottom needle over strand of yarn on finger (top strand), around and under yarn and back up, making a loop around needle. Pull loop snug. Bring top needle (with slipknot) over yarn tail on thumb (bottom strand), around and under yarn and back up, making a loop around needle. Pull loop snug. Cont casting on sts until desired number is reached; top yarn strand always wraps around bottom needle, and bottom yarn strand always wraps around top needle. A tutorial can be found at https:// tutorials.knitpicks.com/judys-magic-cast-on.

Stretchy Bind Off
Directions: K2, *insert LH needle into front of 2 sts on RH needle and knit them tog—1 st remains on RH needle. K1; rep from * until all sts have been bound off. A tutorial can be found at https://tutorials.knitpicks.com/go-your-own- way-socks-toe-up-part-7-binding-off.

Jeny's Surprisingly Stretchy Bind Off (for 1x1 Rib)
Directions: Reverse YO, K1, pass YO over; *YO, P1, pass YO and previous st over P1; reverse YO, K1, pass YO and previous st over K1; rep from * until 1 st is left, then break working yarn and pull it through final st to complete BO.

Kitchener Stitch (also called Grafting)
Seamlessly join two sets of live stitches together.
Directions: With an equal number of sts on two needles, break yarn leaving a tail approx four times as long as the row of sts, and thread through a blunt yarn needle. Hold needles parallel with WSs facing in and both needles pointing to the right. Perform Step 2 on the first front st, then Step 4 on the first back st, then continue from Step 1, always pulling yarn tightly so the grafted row tension matches the knitted fabric:
Step 1: Pull yarn needle K-wise through front st and drop st from knitting needle.
Step 2: Pull yarn needle P-wise through next front st, leaving st on knitting needle.
Step 3: Pull yarn needle P-wise through first back st and drop st from knitting needle.
Step 4: Pull yarn needle K-wise through next back st, leaving st on knitting needle.
Rep Steps 1-4 until all sts have been grafted together, finishing by working Step 1 through the last remaining front st, then Step 3 through the last remaining back st. A tutorial can be found at https://tutorials.knitpicks.com /kitchener-stitch.

Short Rows
There are several options for how to handle short rows, so you may see different suggestions/intructions in a pattern.
Wrap and Turn (W&T) (one option for Short Rows)
Work until the st to be wrapped. If knitting: Bring yarn to front, Sl next st P-wise, return yarn to back; turn work, and Sl wrapped st onto RH needle. Cont across row. If purling: Bring yarn to back of work, Sl next st P-wise, return yarn to front; turn work and Sl wrapped st onto RH needle. Cont across row.
Picking up Wraps: Work to wrapped st. If knitting: Insert RH needle under wrap, then through wrapped st K-wise; K st and wrap tog. If purling: Sl wrapped st P-wise onto RH needle, use LH needle to lift wrap and place it onto RH needle; Sl wrap and st back onto LH needle, and P tog.
A tutorial for W&T can be found at https://tutorials.knitpicks .com/short-rows-wrap-and-turn-or-wt.
German Short Rows (another option for Short Rows)
Work to turning point; turn. WYIF, Sl first st P-wise. Bring yarn over back of right needle, pulling firmly to create a "double stitch" on RH needle. If next st is a K st, leave yarn at back; if next st is a P st, bring yarn to front between needles. When it's time to work into double st, knit both strands tog.

THIS COLLECTION FEATURES

Aloft™
Lace Weight
72% Super Kid Mohair, 28% Silk

Alpaca Cloud™
Fingering Weight
100% Superfine Alpaca

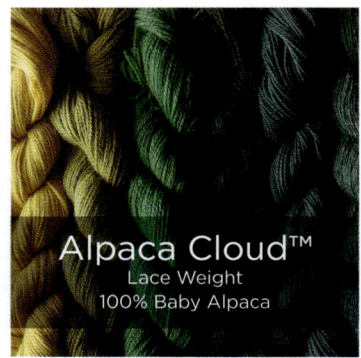

Alpaca Cloud™
Lace Weight
100% Baby Alpaca

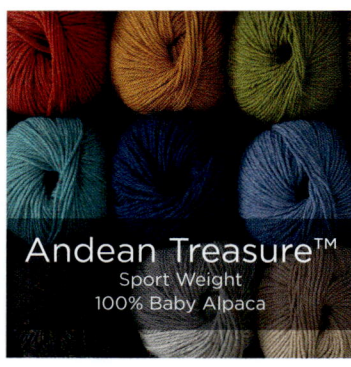

Andean Treasure™
Sport Weight
100% Baby Alpaca

Capra™
DK Weight
85% Fine Merino Wool, 15% Cashmere

Capretta™ Superwash
Fingering Weight
80% Fine Superwash Merino Wool,
10% Cashmere, 10% Nylon

Gloss™ Lace
Lace Weight
70% Merino Wool, 30% Silk

Paragon™
Sport Weight
50% Fine Merino Wool, 25% Baby
Alpaca, 25% Mulberry Silk

View these beautiful
yarns and more at
www.KnitPicks.com

Knit Picks yarn is both luxe and affordable—a seeming contradiction
trounced! But it's not just about the pretty colors; we also care
deeply about fiber quality and fair labor practices, leaving you with
a gorgeously reliable product you'll turn to time and time again.